50 FINDS
FROM HAMPSHIRE
Objects from the Portable
Antiquities Scheme

Katie Hinds

AMBERLEY

First published 2017

Amberley Publishing
The Hill, Stroud
Gloucestershire, GL5 4EP

www.amberley-books.com

Copyright © Katie Hinds, 2017

The right of Katie Hinds to be identified as the
Author of this work has been asserted in accordance
with the Copyrights, Designs and Patents Act 1988.

ISBN 978 1 4456 6234 3 (print)
ISBN 978 1 4456 6235 0 (ebook)

British Library Cataloguing in Publication Data.
A catalogue record for this book is available from
the British Library.

Typeset in 10pt on 13pt Celeste.
Origination by Amberley Publishing.
Printed in the UK.

Contents

Acknowledgements

This book could not have been written without the many metal detectorists who record their finds with the Portable Antiquities Scheme. For not only the ability to write this book, but for helping to record our history for posterity, to them I am indebted. Thank you.

Many of the '50 Finds' discussed here were recorded by Portable Antiquities Scheme colleagues and, without their wonderful work, I would have struggled to accomplish the book. Of particular note are previous Hampshire Finds Liaison Officers Sally Worrell, Jodi Puls and Rob Webley, as well as other colleagues too numerous to mention here but who are credited on the PAS database.

Tracking down enough images of the right objects has been a tricky task and I am immensely grateful to colleagues both local and further afield for giving their time to help me, in particular Mark Barden, Dave Allen, Ross Turle, Wendy Bowen, Robin Iles, Sally Worrell, Ciorstaidh Hayward Trevarthen, Lisa Brown, Jane Ellis-Schön and Pippa Bradley. Thank you also to Ronnie Robb for coming to my aid with his illustrative skills.

Thank you so much to those who gave up their evenings and weekends to read the various drafts of text for the book – David Williams, Dot Boughton, Dave Allen, Rob Webley, Sally Worrell and Marion Hinds. The book has been vastly improved with your valuable input!

Thank you too to Alan Whitney for helping me visualise Hampshire's geology.

I owe a debt of gratitude to colleagues Dot Boughton, David Williams, Jo Ahmet, Sally Worrell, Rob Webley, Dave Allen and Neil Wilkin for their specialist input in the interpretation of the finds discussed. I hope I have done them justice.

A special thank you goes to Peter Reavill for using his QGIS mapping expertise to create maps of all the finds discussed in the book.

The reproductions of a number of images are by the kind permission of David Williams, Dot Boughton, Mike Trevarthen, Hampshire Cultural Trust, The Wiltshire Museum, Devizes, The Salisbury Museum and Wessex Archaeology. Unless otherwise stated, all other images are courtesy of the Portable Antiquities Scheme. Every attempt has been made to seek permission for copyright material used in this book. However, if we have inadvertently used copyright material without permission/acknowledgement we apologise and we will make the necessary correction at the first opportunity.

Thanks are extended to my employer, Hampshire Cultural Trust, which hosts the Hampshire Finds Liaison Officer post with support from Hampshire County Council, Winchester City Council, Southampton City Council and the New Forest National Park Authority.

More generally, thank you to all my friends, family and colleagues who have supported me during the writing of this book and who are too numerous to mention here.

A final thank you goes to my non-archaeological husband Craig Robb for his patience, advice and IT skills, and for driving me around many Hampshire sites, enabling me to hang out of the window to take photographs.

Foreword by Michael Lewis

The places in which we live and work have a long past, but one that is not always obvious in the landscape around us. This is a forgotten past. Most of us know little about the people who once lived in our communities fifty years ago, let alone 500, or even 5,000 years past. Like us, they lived, played and worked here, in this place, but we know almost nothing of them ...

History books tell us about royalty, great lords and important churchmen, but most others are forgotten by time. The only evidence for many of these people is the objects that they left behind; sometimes buried on purpose, but more often lost by chance. Occasionally, through archaeological fieldwork, we can place these objects in a context that allows us to better understand the past, but nowadays excavation is mostly development led, so only takes place when a new building, road or service pipe, is being constructed.

A unique way of understanding the past is through the finds recorded through the Portable Antiquities Scheme of which those chosen here by Katie Hinds (Hampshire Finds Liaison Officer) are just fifty of over 43,000 from Hampshire on its database (www.finds.org.uk). These finds are all discovered by the public, most by metal-detector users, searching in places archaeologists are unlikely to go or otherwise excavate. As such, they provide important clues of underlying archaeology that (once recorded) help archaeologists understand our past – a past of the people, found by the people.

Some of these finds are truly magnificent, others less imposing. Yet, like pieces in a jigsaw puzzle, they are often meaningless alone, but once placed together paint a picture. These finds therefore allow us to understand the story of people who once lived here, in Hampshire.

Dr Michael Lewis
Head of Portable Antiquities & Treasure
British Museum

Introduction

The Portable Antiquities Scheme (PAS) is a scheme for the voluntary recording of archaeological objects found by members of the public, especially metal detectorists, but also dog walkers, field walkers and those who make discoveries while digging their garden. It was the brainchild of Dr Roger Bland (formerly of the British Museum) and inspired by existing models in East Anglia, where archaeologists had been recording metal detector finds since the 1970s. Hampshire was introduced to the scheme in 1999 as part of a second pilot project; the scheme eventually went national in 2003, with almost every county being covered by one Finds Liaison Officer (FLO). Wales have their own FLO. While England and Wales are the first European countries to offer such recording schemes, Scotland has a similar scheme and, excitingly, recording schemes are now being established in Denmark, Belgium and the Netherlands.

The PAS was launched on the back of the 1996 Treasure Act, which came into force in September 1997 (a summary of the definition of Treasure can be found on the PAS website: www.finds.org.uk/treasure). There is an obligation to report finds of potential Treasure to the local coroner within fourteen days of discovery, and the PAS acts as an intermediary in this process – a number of the finds in this book have been subject to the Treasure process.

Non-treasure finds, in comparison, are far more numerous but of no less importance historically, and the PAS is interested in recording all man-made finds, no matter how fragmentary, from the prehistoric period to the seventeenth century. These are recorded on the PAS online database (www.finds.org.uk/database) with as precise a findspot as possible and no less than a six-figure national grid reference (accurate to 100 x 100 m). Arguably, the findspot is the most important aspect of any find – once we know where it was found, an object tells a much more detailed story.

To date (August 2016), 483 research projects have utilised PAS data – these are a mixture of school projects, undergraduate and postgraduate research, projects run by local history societies and desk-based assessments from Historic Environment Records. However, the database can be used by anyone with internet access.

The majority of finders are metal detectorists, many of whom feel very strongly about the importance of recording their finds and contributing to the knowledge of our past. They follow a code of practice for responsible detecting, working only in the plough soil, so as not to disturb any unknown archaeology, and offering all their finds for recording with detailed findspot information. Metal detectorists are also valuable finders of worked flint and pottery. Many of the finds discussed below have been found by metal detectorists, but some have been chance finds by members of the public in gardens and elsewhere; one has been recorded onto the database by its finder, who is a volunteer recorder for the PAS.

Hampshire is one of Britain's southernmost counties, bounded to the west, north and east by Dorset, Wiltshire, Berkshire, Surrey and West Sussex, while its southern border is the Solent and English Channel. This connection with the sea (in much earlier times a land bridge existed to northern Europe) provided a vital trade link and entry point into Britain from prehistoric times to the present day. The growing interest in Hampshire's past was cemented in 1885 with the birth of the Hampshire Field Club. Since then, an incredible amount of archaeological work has been done in the county, from the efforts of the early collectors and recorders, such as Heywood Sumner, J. P. Williams-Freeman and George Willis, to the great research excavation projects directed by academics like Barry Cunliffe, Martin Biddle and Mike Fulford. The story continues today, with a vibrant picture of 'developer-led' archaeology across the area.

Hampshire's geology must, by its nature, dictate settlement patterns and industry to a considerable degree. The very north of the county, as well as the Solent and New Forest, are on the Upper and Lower Eocene layer of clay, silt and sand, with an area to the south and east of Brockenhurst on the more recent Oligocene deposits. The area in between comprises the Chalk, part of which is the South Downs National Park, which then extends eastwards into Sussex. Topographically, the county's highest points are along the northern and eastern edges of the Chalk Downs (Linkenholt to Odiham, then south to Privett), the area beyond to the very east (Petersfield and north) being a Greensand layer of mudstone and sandstone. While the PAS has recorded finds from across Hampshire, the greatest number comes from the chalk. While this tallies with much of what we know of settlement patterns (the chalk and its river valleys being good land for farming), it should also be noted that it is indicative of where people go metal detecting (the land still being well-cultivated today). Areas such as the New Forest, much of which is woodland and part of a protected National Park, see much less metal detection.

Today, Hampshire is a largely rural county, with a conurbation along its coastal line connecting two of its three cities, Southampton and Portsmouth. At its heart lies the county town, the city of Winchester. The three cities are famously known for their place in history, but alongside them are many smaller and larger towns, villages and hamlets, all of which have their origins in our past. In the last twenty years or so, archaeological investigation has focused very much on development, and therefore urban areas, so the PAS and its finders (mostly working in the rural countryside) contribute a huge amount of information about these smaller, lesser-known places and sometimes find evidence of locations now lost to us. Recently, however, the countryside surrounding Winchester, Andover and Basingstoke has begun to be lost to the developers, and what was once the preserve of the detectorist is now being explored by the contract archaeologist. In the case of one development in Winchester, this has led to successful collaboration between archaeologists and metal detectorists.

The finds discussed below are my personal choice. In choosing the finds, I have tried to focus on not only those that are outstanding, made of precious metal or of national importance, but also on the more typical, everyday finds we see. These are usually made of base metals, pottery or stone and are often of domestic or personal use. All finds have a tale to tell and also the potential to enhance the knowledge of our past.

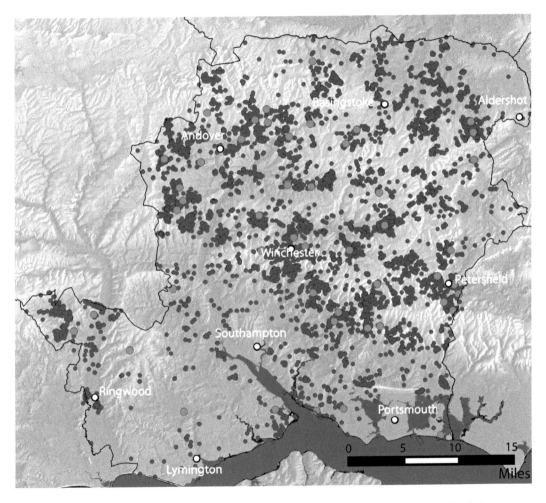

Map of Hampshire showing the distribution of the fifty finds discussed in this book (in red) on top of all the finds recorded for the county by the PAS (in blue).

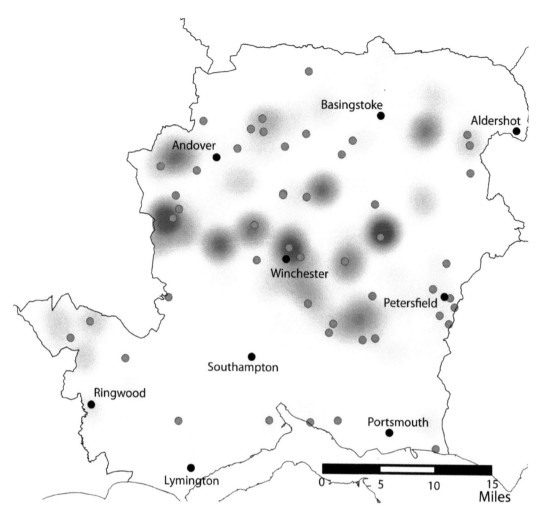

A 'heat density' map, showing concentrations of all Hampshire finds recorded by the PAS – the brighter the colour, the greater the number of finds recorded. The fifty finds discussed in this book are red dots.

Chapter 1
The Stone Age in Hampshire

The Stone Age can be subdivided into the Palaeolithic, Mesolithic and Neolithic periods, which translate to the old, middle and new Stone Ages, and covers a vast number of years, from 500,000 to 2400 BC. The finds the PAS sees from this period are occasionally of pottery (which, if disturbed by the plough, break up very easily) but more usually of stone. In Hampshire this is in the medium of flint, thanks to the copious natural deposits in the county. Indeed, Hampshire was home to flint mines at Martin Down at Over Wallop on the Upper Chalk geological band, which have a radiocarbon date of around 3100 BC.

We see evidence of the earliest Stone Age, the Palaeolithic (500,000–8000 BC), mainly through flint hand axes and flakes. Their distribution follows the river valleys and coastline (with major sites at Dunbridge, Colden Common, Rainbow Bar and Warsash), to some extent reflecting the movement of early people into Britain. Hampshire provides a greater corpus of Palaeolithic finds than other, more inland areas of the UK, but even so these are still small in number given the huge timescales involved. We owe much of our present knowledge of this period to the reviewing and plotting of finds by the English Rivers Palaeolithic Project (supported by English Heritage), which was published in 1999.

In the Mesolithic period (8000–4000 BC) we largely encounter waste flakes (debitage), along with microliths (tiny worked blades as part of a composite tool) and tranchet axe heads (with chisel-like cutting ends). Excavated Hampshire sites include Langstone Harbour, Braishfield and Longmoor Inclosure, Whitehill.

The Neolithic (4000–2400 BC) is represented in the landscape by long barrows (burial mounds), which form groups in several different areas of the chalk. Tools of varying shapes and purpose emerge, and the polished axe is introduced. Some of these are of very fine quality but are unwieldy in size; they were probably intended for ritual rather than for chopping and trimming trees.

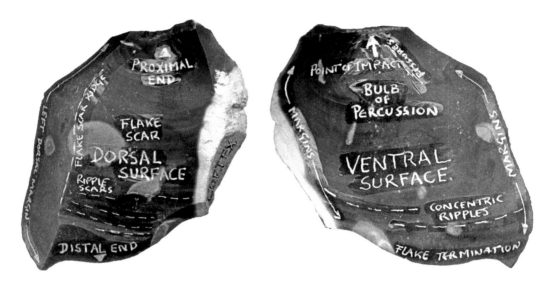

Struck flake, detailing the different features to look out for when recording worked flint. A bulb of percussion and concentric ripples are a good sign that a flake has been intentionally removed from its core.

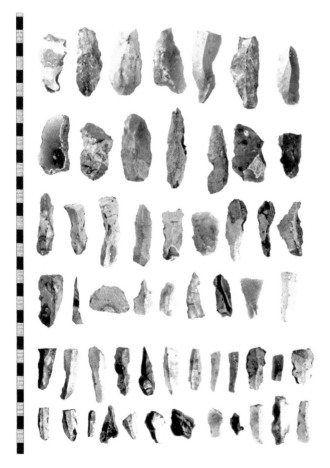

A collection of late Mesolithic or Early Neolithic struck flint blades and flakes from Havant. (IOW-A3D1A4)

1. Flint hand axe (HAMP-222E28)
Lower Palaeolithic (500,000–250,000 BC)
Found in Warnford in the 1950s. Length 122.5 mm.

This hand axe was discovered by a boy playing in the river at the bottom of his garden. It was treasured for many years before being brought in for recording in 2013. Hand axes, as the name suggests, would have been held in the hand and were primarily used for butchery. In Hampshire, Palaeolithic finds cluster along the south coast and the main river valleys, this hand axe being from the River Meon. It is oval and has had flakes removed from both faces to shape it. The flint has patinated to a distinct orange or 'toffee' colour, which is often indicative of Palaeolithic date.

Lower Palaeolithic
flint hand axe
from Warnford.

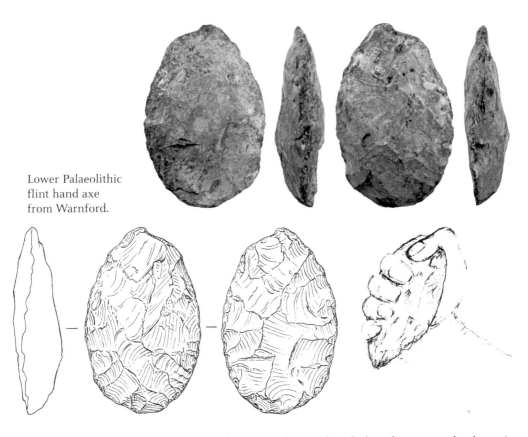

Left: Lower Palaeolithic flint hand axe from Warnford. Although the colour cannot be shown in the same way as a photograph, a line drawing depicts the depth of the object more successfully. (Illustration by Mike Trevarthen)

Right: Artist's drawing, showing a hand axe in use. (Illustration by Ronnie Robb)

13

Named after a site in northern France, Levallois-Perret, the Levallois tool is created using a specific method of core preparation so that, when a flake is struck, it has ready-sharp edges and only needs minimal additional work to make it good for use. This example is shaped like a teardrop and, like find no. 1, is of the distinctive 'toffee' colour of the Palaeolithic period. The areas of lighter colour represent more recent damage. Noticeable on this flake are its smooth, rounded edges – this suggests it has been 'rolled' in a high-energy environment (such as a river) before its final deposition.

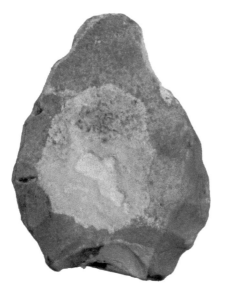

Above: Middle Palaeolithic flint Levallois flake from Titchfield.

Left: Three distinctive 'tortoise shell' (shaped) flint cores from Northamptonshire; their surfaces are prepared in this way for the production of tools such as blades and scrapers. Such cores are characteristic of Levallois-style tool production. (NARC-56E1B7)

3. Flint adze (HAMP-594273)
Mesolithic (8000–4000 BC)
Found on Hayling Island in 1986. Length 161 mm.

Unlike the earlier hand axe, the adzes and axes from the Mesolithic period onwards would have been hafted to a wooden or antler handle and primarily used for woodworking. This adze has an asymmetrical hexagonal cross section, the upper and lower surfaces thickening where the other thins and vice versa. At the tip are several long flake scars, with further short removals at the very edge, possibly for sharpening. The flint is grey in colour, with patches of orange iron staining.

An adze chops in a vertical action, as opposed to the more horizontal plane of an axe. The blade of the adze is mounted perpendicular to the handle.

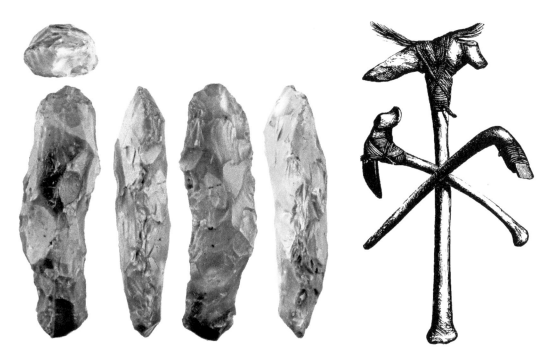

Left: Mesolithic flint adze from Hayling Island.

Right: Nineteenth-century interpretation of a contemporary hafted adze (far right in image). (J. Evans, 1872; *The Ancient Stone Implements, Weapons and Ornaments of Great Britain*)

4. Greenstone axe head (HAMP-008C86)
Neolithic (4000–2400 BC)
Found in St Mary Bourne in 2013. Length 138.9 mm.

During the Neolithic period, the landscape transformed dramatically as the people of Hampshire left behind their hunter-gatherer lifestyle and became farmers. This change brought with it the introduction of new tools, and finds from this period are more common than those from the Mesolithic and Palaeolithic periods. The chalk downlands of Hampshire were a useful source of flint for Stone Age man. However, axes made of other types of stone are occasionally found. These have often been traded over considerable distances and some were probably prized possessions. For example, a jadeite axe, now in the Wiltshire Museum, Devizes, was discovered in Breamore but came from the Italian Alps. It is likely that it was manufactured there, too. This example from St Mary Bourne is made of greenstone, a type of stone found in Devon and Cornwall around the edges of the granite intrusions that form Dartmoor, Bodmin Moor and Lands End. The axe head is triangular, with a badly damaged cutting edge. The stone is grey-green in colour with a number of white inclusions, typical of a metamorphosed igneous rock.

Above: Neolithic jadeite axe found in Breamore. (Wiltshire Museum, Devizes)

Left: Neolithic greenstone axe head from St Mary Bourne.

5. Flint discoidal knife (WILT-B18965)
Later Neolithic/ Early Bronze Age (2700–1500 BC)
Found in Rockbourne in 2009. Length 77.8 mm.

A particularly unusual tool type is this discoidal knife, which may have had an alternative use as a scraper. It has two flat faces and rounded ends, which were produced through repeated grinding and polishing – a sophisticated technique, associated with the Neolithic and axe heads in particular. To achieve this shiny, glass-like surface, it would have taken a specialist many hours of work. A polished surface does not improve the function of the object, however – the amount of work that went into producing the surface strongly suggests that aesthetics played a vital role in the manufacture of this specimen. This knife is made from a grey flint and has had its very edges polished to a point, flanked by a bevelled, polished border. It was damaged in antiquity and reworked in several places (along the jagged end as well as one of the long edges) so that it could be reused.

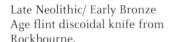

Late Neolithic/ Early Bronze Age flint discoidal knife from Rockbourne.

This very large, 152 mm long, polished axe head from West Yorkshire would have been a prized possession and may not have seen much use, its value perhaps existing instead as an item of gift exchange. (SWYOR-328703)

Chapter 2
The Bronze Age in Hampshire

The Bronze Age in Britain dates from between 2,400 to 800 BC. It is the time when we see the introduction of metals such as gold, copper and tin. Due to their durability and good survival in the ground, we see a vast expansion of object types throughout the Bronze Age.

The earliest phase of the Bronze Age is sometimes known as the Chalcolithic, or Copper Age, and marks the transition from the Late Neolithic into the Early Bronze Age between 2500 and 2200 BC. It is also known as the 'Beaker period' after a distinctive form of pottery. Metal finds from this date are of copper or gold and are fairly rare. Two Beaker-period graves, in the same burial monument, were excavated near Chilbolton in 1986. Both contained a beaker, but one had, in addition, two pairs of gold basket ornaments, a gold bead, a copper knife, fifty-five stone beads and an assortment of flint flakes.

A Wessex/ Middle Rhine Beaker found with a male crouched burial at Kempshott Park, Basingstoke, in 2000. A radiocarbon date on the bone calibrates to 2210–2020 BC. The vessel is 152 mm in height. (Hampshire County Council; provided by Hampshire Cultural Trust)

The finds from the Chilbolton beaker grave group on display at Andover Museum. (Hampshire County Council; provided by Hampshire Cultural Trust)

The Early Bronze Age (2400–1500 BC) in Hampshire is characterised in the landscape by its round barrows (burial mounds). These took various forms – disc, bell and bowl barrows are all known – but many are now ploughed flat and recognisable only by their ditches. They tend to cluster in the New Forest, the north-east of the county and parts of the chalk downlands, although they can be found right across Hampshire. Barrow cemeteries can be seen at Old Winchester Hill, Petersfield Heath and Burghclere (to either side of the A34).

The Middle Bronze Age (1500–1100 BC) is characterised by a new form of axe head, the palstave, which, in addition to the side flanges, now has a stop ridge added to its middle section to improve the position and stability of the haft. We also see the introduction of the rapier, a narrow-bladed weapon. The Middle Bronze Age is also known for the introduction of many metal ornaments, not just made of gold, which is why it is often referred to as 'Ornament Horizon'. Structurally perhaps the most fascinating discovery of the period are the waterlogged remains of several timber bridges from Testwood Lake, Eling, excavated between 1996 and 1999 by Wessex Archaeology.

Settlement and other structures of the Late Bronze Age (1100–800 BC) are little known, although large pre-hillfort enclosures were created at Winklebury (Basingstoke), Balkesbury and Danebury. It is, however, relatively prolific in terms of its metalwork compared with the earlier periods. Finds of tools such as gouges, knives, chisels and axe heads, along with weapons of swords and spears, occur as single finds as well as in large metalwork hoards, in which they are often associated with copper ingots for presumed reworking. These are sometimes known as Founder's hoards.

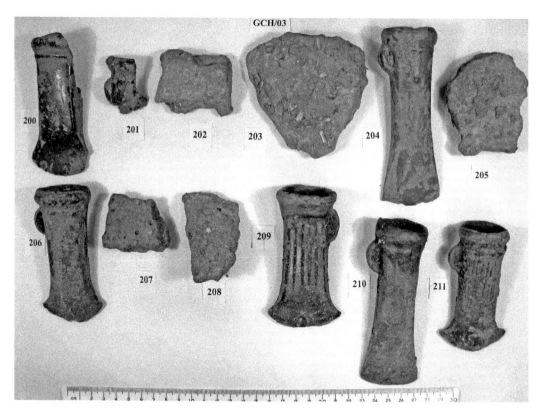

Late Bronze Age Founder's hoard of socketed axes and bronze ingots, acquired by Maidstone Museum through the Treasure Act. (KENT-757FC0)

Evolution of the bronze axe, from left to right: Early Bronze Age flat axe (HESH-D95656), Middle Bronze Age palstave (HAMP-B0D6B5), Late Bronze Age socketed axe (WILT-A30E3C).

6. Gold jewellery (BERK-F548E6)
Earliest Bronze Age or Chalcolithic (2400–2200 BC)
Found in Whitchurch in 2015. Ornament 1 length: 35.9 mm; Ornament 2
length: 32.0 mm.

These two very rare sheet-gold objects date from the earliest phase of metallurgy in Britain. They were found folded one inside the other, presumably intentionally. Ornament 1 is incomplete, with a folded rectangular tang projecting from one edge and decorated, on one side only, with incised lines and punched dots. Ornament 2 (which was folded inside ornament 1) is complete and relatively undamaged. A short, pierced tab projects from one edge and the decoration is similar to that on the first piece, though some incised lines are not well executed and it may have been reused and reshaped.

Such objects are referred to as 'basket ornaments', as they were rolled into a distinctive basket shape (the examples here have been unrolled post-discovery). They are generally interpreted as objects of personal adornment and perhaps used as earrings or hair tresses. These two basket ornaments from Whitchurch are the eighth pair to be discovered in Britain, including the two pairs discovered at Chilbolton (discussed above in the introduction to this chapter) and a pair each from the graves of the 'Archer' and the 'Archer's Companion' in Amesbury, Wiltshire. The Whitchurch and Chilbolton examples are important discoveries for our understanding of Hampshire during the Bronze Age, which has seemed poor in comparison with the numerous rich burials from neighbouring Wiltshire.

The Whitchurch basket ornaments were declared Treasure and subsequently donated by the landowner and finder to Hampshire Cultural Trust.

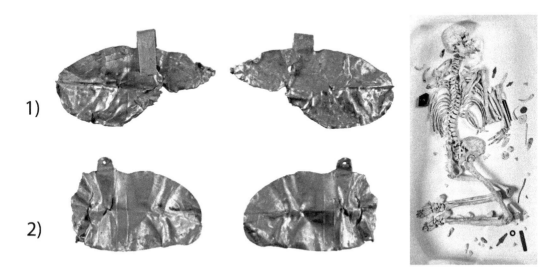

Left: Earliest Bronze Age gold jewellery from Whitchurch.

Right: The 'Amesbury Archer' and his grave goods on display in The Salisbury Museum. (National Geographic)

The Amesbury Archer's gold basket ornaments. (National Geographic)

'The Amesbury Archer' by Jane Brayne. (Wessex Archaeology)

7. Flint barbed-and-tanged arrowhead (PUBLIC-279713)
Early Bronze Age (2400–1500 BC)
Found in Petersfield in 2014. Length 27 mm.

Even though the Bronze Age saw the introduction of metals for most tool and weapon types, arrowheads continued to be made from flint. This barbed-and-tanged arrowhead is struck from a mid-grey flint with a square tang and barbs, roughly the same length as each other. Both faces have been skillfully pressure-flaked to produce this finely crafted piece. Similar flint barbed-and-tanged arrowheads are associated with the Beaker phase of the Early Bronze Age.

There are known examples of copper-alloy arrowheads of barbed-and-tanged form, but these are extremely rare finds and one has not yet been found in a dateable context. It is tempting, however, to liken their form to the Early Bronze Age flint types.

Early Bronze Age flint
barbed-and-tanged arrowhead.

A copper-alloy barbed-and-tanged
arrowhead from Lincolnshire.
(SWYOR-3A2CF7)

8. Bronze hoard (SUR-9A711C)
Middle Bronze Age (1400–1250 BC)
Found in Buriton in 2016. Diameters: Torc 1 – 180 mm; Torc 2 – 187 mm;
Armlet 1 – 87 mm; Armlet 2 – 84 mm.

Soft copper, which we see in the very early phases of the Bronze Age, is eventually mixed with tin to create the much stronger bronze. By the Middle Bronze Age we begin to see the objects of the Ornament Horizon: adornments of the fingers, wrists and neck. This particular hoard comprises two spiral-twisted torcs and two bracelets or armrings. Neither the torcs nor the bracelets form matching pairs, although they are similar in size and form.

Torc 1 has forty-three twisted ridges and is missing one hooked terminal, while Torc 2 has seventy-seven twisted ridges with both terminals intact. The bracelets are both circular in form but are significantly different in colour, which suggests that they were made from different alloys. Bracelet 1 has extensive incised herring-bone decoration and other patterns, while the other is similarly decorated but with less detail.

The finder reported that each bracelet was placed inside a torc, and that the two pairs were separated by a layer of earth. This structured form of deposition is consistent with other Ornament Horizon hoards from southern England. This is the ninth Ornament Horizon hoard from Hampshire and the sixth to contain bracelets/armrings. A hoard from South Wonston contains both an annular bracelet and a spiral-twisted torc.

Middle Bronze Age hoard from Buriton.

Bracelet/armlet 1.

Bracelet/armlet 2.

Detail of the twisted ridge decoration on one of the torcs. Soil still adheres to the surface.

9. Bronze scabbard chape (HAMP-095061)
Late Bronze Age (900–800 BC)
Found in Quarley in 2009. Length 35.7 mm.

The Late Bronze Age brought with it more diversity in tools, weaponry and ornaments. This particular object would have been both functional and decorative. It is a chape, which would have adorned the end of the leather scabbard into which a sword or dagger would have been placed, both to protect the weapon and the wearer. This type is known as 'bag-shaped' and tends to be confined to south-east England and northern France, with a few known from Ireland. It has a rounded bottom and a raised border at the damaged attachment end, and is decorated with three punched ring-and-dot motifs to either side. The metal is a mid-green in colour with traces of corrosion in the punched dots.

Left: Late Bronze Age scabbard chape from Quarley.

Right: Of similar age but of a different shape and much larger size (205 mm in length), this scabbard chape from Somerset is presumably for a sword. It was acquired by Somerset County Museum. (SOMDOR-9ADF54)

10. Gold penannular ring (SUR-7A1338)
Late Bronze Age (1100–750 BC)
Found in Old Alresford in 2011. Diameter 15.6 mm.

This object is an ornament, but it has become known colloquially as 'ring money', although it is unknown whether penannular rings ever played a part in trade and exchange. It is perhaps more likely that it was an object of body adornment, perhaps worn on the nose, ears or in the hair. Such rings can be solid gold or have copper cores. Some are plain while others are decorated, as in this example, with the addition of a thin strip of contrasting metal alloy wound around and across it to produce a striped effect. The PAS has recorded over 100 to date, mostly from southern, central and eastern England. This example was acquired by Winchester Museum (now Hampshire Cultural Trust) after being declared Treasure under the Treasure Act.

Late Bronze Age gold penannular ring from Old Alresford.

A penannular ring from Rockbourne with a copper-alloy core, the corrosion product visibly leaching from the terminals and areas of the surface. Diameter 15.6 mm. (WILT-36F326)

This solid gold penannular armlet was an isolated find at a high point in the landscape and close to a water source, a pattern we see in the deposition of Late Bronze Age hoards. It is likely that the armlet's deposition had a special purpose. Even towards the end of the Bronze Age, when gold artefacts are generally more numerous (and display new techniques and types), they are still unusual discoveries. This armlet is undecorated. It has a circular cross-section and expanded, dished terminals.

Three very similar armlets with expanded terminals are known from a hoard at Selsey in West Sussex. This perhaps suggests the existence of a local workshop, given the relative proximity to the Hampshire discovery.

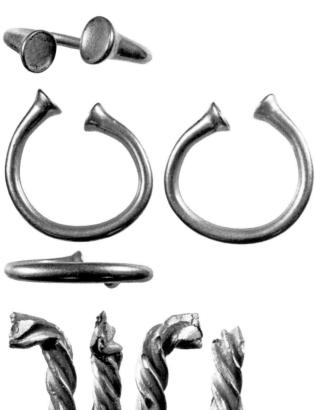

Late Bronze Age gold armlet from Soberton.

This fragment of gold torc or armlet from Droxford is earlier in date and comes from the 'Ornament Horizon' of the Middle Bronze Age. It features bar-twisted decoration. Length 20.8 mm. (HAMP-C8DC02)

The owner of this find had acquired it with his house, and it had an accompanying note to say it was thought to have been found in the 1970s in the Lymington River. As with the previous object, it is likely that this was an intentional deposition rather than a loss, and it is quite common to find Bronze Age objects in watery locations (or locations that were watery in Bronze Age times). Indeed, it is so common that, when Late Bronze Age hoards and penannular rings are overlain on a map of Britain's waterways, the finds closely follow the watercourses.

The plain pegged spearhead has a leaf-shaped blade, which has chamfered edges and a pronounced mid-rib. The spear would have been attached to a shaft at its socketed end and further secured with rivets in the peg holes. It is likely that it was used for hunting.

Late Bronze Age spear
from Brockenhurst.

This Middle/Late Bronze Age rapier from Oxfordshire has perhaps been ritually deposited – it was intentionally destroyed before burial by being broken in two. Length 234 mm. (GLO-036A39)

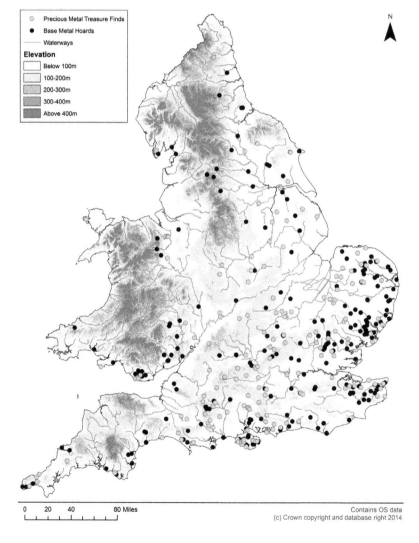

A map of Britain's rivers showing Bronze Age precious metal finds and base metal hoards. (Sally Worrell/Katherine Robbins)

Chapter 3
The Iron Age in Hampshire

The Iron Age runs from 800 BC and overlaps with the Roman invasion of Britain in AD 43. Visually, the Iron Age in Hampshire is represented by its many hillforts (including Danebury, Beacon Hill and Old Winchester Hill). These likely acted not only as settlements but also as secure storage sites during their heyday in the early and middle period. However, it becomes clear that, towards the end of the Iron Age, it is the *oppida* (or tribal capitals) of Venta and Calleva (Winchester and Silchester) that are the new focus for settlement. There is also evidence for a late Iron Age temple on Hayling Island, suggesting connection at the time with the settlement complex that was to become Noviomagus (Chichester) in Roman times, which lies within sight of it.

A common find of the very earliest Iron Age are bronze socketed axe heads in an unfinished state, sometimes with a high tin content, which would make them useless as a cutting tool. They are often deposited in great numbers in metalwork hoards. A number of single finds are known from Hampshire and discussed further in find no. 12 below. The finds we typically see from the earlier Iron Age are (occasionally) pottery and (more frequently) bronze metalwork, not iron as it survives so poorly in the ground. Iron, which is harder and gives a sharper edge, is likely to have been favoured for the manufacture of axes and weaponry, while bronze became the preferred metal for smaller and more ornate objects. The Iron Age is renowned for its beautifully moulded brooches and harness fittings, which were often inlaid with coral or enamel. The large number of Iron Age harness and chariot fittings strongly indicates the increasing significance of horses, horse-drawn carts and chariots.

During the later Iron Age, the first coinage in Britain appears. In Hampshire the coins we see are made mostly from precious metal (gold and silver). These coins are also valuable indicators of the tribal boundaries within the county – the Durotriges to the west, the Atrebates and Regini in the north and east, while the area between may have belonged to a tribe called the Belgae. We have also recorded a large number of Continental coins from Hampshire for this period, which emphasise a strong cross-channel connection with Iron Age communities in northern France and Belgium.

Danebury Iron Age hillfort from the air. (Hampshire Data Portal via Wikimedia Commons)

A Middle Iron Age brooch from Andover, missing coral or enamel settings. (HAMP-2B6848)

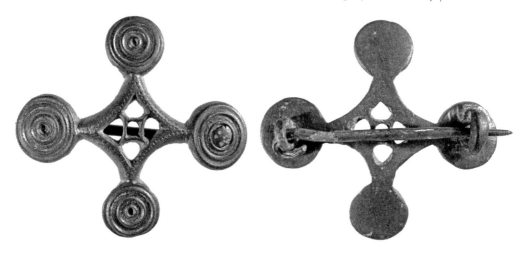

A Middle Iron Age brooch from Wiltshire with a contemporary catchplate repair, visible to the front as a domed green 'setting'. (WILT-E2D3B2)

13. **Hoard of Armorican bronze socketed axe heads (HAMP1485, for example)**
Earliest Iron Age (800–600 BC)
Found in Fawley in 2000. Typical length *c.* 130 mm.

After the development of the axe head as an essential tool during the Stone Age and Bronze Age, we see an interesting phenomenon develop at the very end of the Bronze Age and the beginning of the Iron Age – the deposition of large hoards of axe heads that have not been used and were probably never intended for use at all. They all feature unsharpened blades and prominent casting seams, and some retain a clay core from the casting process. While there are several British types of these axes, hoards of Armorican axes (Armorica being roughly the area of modern-day Brittany) have been found in Cornwall, the Isle of Wight and Hampshire. Hoards of Armorican axes found in north-western France are often enormous in size; our local hoard from Fawley is rather more modest at sixty-eight in number. It is the third Armorican axe hoard from Hampshire. The axe heads are undecorated, with almost parallel sides and a single loop. It is likely that they were deposited for ritual purpose or safekeeping.

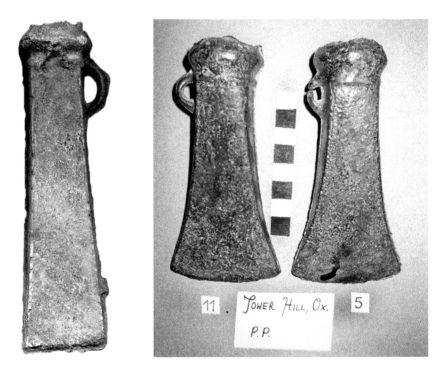

Left: One of a hoard of sixty-eight earliest Iron Age Armorican axes from Fawley.

Right: Two axes from the Tower Hill hoard from Oxfordshire. Not only have the casting flashes not been trimmed, but the shiny colour of the metal suggests that it has a high tin content. This would look spectacular but would have made the metal softer, and therefore useless as a tool. (Dot Boughton)

14. Copper-alloy toggle (HAMP-85188B)
Iron Age (300 BC–AD 100)
Found near Petersfield in 2014. Length 30.2 mm.

A functional and highly decorative object, this toggle would have fastened two sections of cloth together, perhaps on a bag or an item of clothing. It is decorated in a style know as La Tène II (after a site on Lake Neuchâtel in Switzerland), with distinctive tendrils curving and swirling in a continuous pattern.

The toggle is formed of two hemispheres, set at an angle to each other, and two large circular collets extending from within, perhaps imitative of eyes (the tiny knops around the edge looking rather like eyelashes). The settings from these collets are missing and, from what we know of other objects in the later La Tène style, it is likely they would have been brightly coloured enamel or coral. A loop for fastening extends to the rear, with a moulded ring-and-dot motif to either side.

Left: Iron Age toggle from Petersfield.

Right: This ring-headed pin is of similar date and function to the toggle, and would have worked as a clothing fastener. A light pink coral roundel can be seen on the front, and enamel decoration is missing at the sides. The sharp bend in the shank is a known feature and thought to aid fastening. From Preston Candover. (HAMP-A3A892)

15. Gold jewellery known as 'The Winchester Hoard' (PAS-845331)
Late Iron Age (75–25 BC)
Found near Winchester in 2000. Torc lengths 480 mm and 440 mm; Knotenfibeln length 60 mm.

The most important find of Iron Age gold in a generation, the Winchester Hoard comprises two pairs of brooches, one gold chain, two penannular bracelets and two torcs or necklaces. One pair of brooches is of a type known as '*Knotenfibeln*', after the distinctive knot-like boss on the bow. Prior to this find, we only knew of bronze examples from south-east England.

One of the brooches was found still attached to the gold chain, the collars of which match the brooch terminals. The second pair of brooches is of a type mostly found in France, but

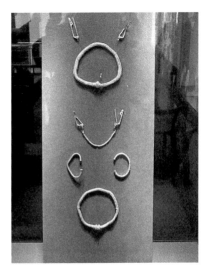

The Winchester Hoard on display at Winchester City Museum in 2002/3. Acquired through the Treasure Act by the British Museum. (Winchester City Council; provided by Hampshire Cultural Trust)

Artistic interpretation of how the jewellery in the Winchester Hoard may have been worn, by Mark Barden. (Winchester City Council; provided by Hampshire Cultural Trust)

again only in bronze. The examples from Winchester would have been attached by a chain, but this was not found. Bronze examples of both types of brooch are relatively common in central and western Europe, but only a dozen or so gold brooches of these types were known before the discovery of the Winchester Hoard.

The two bracelets are undecorated and, when compared with the fine detailing on the brooches and torcs, they seem rather plain. It has been suggested that they might instead be ingots.

By far the most fascinating objects in the hoard are the two necklaces; one is larger, perhaps for a man, and one is smaller, with filigree decoration on the terminals, maybe worn by his female companion. Both show clear signs of wear. Although clearly influenced by the Iron Age torc, these necklaces are not rigid but made of flexible chain, a type of craftsmanship only seen in Rome or Hellenistic Greece at the time. They are unparalleled in Europe north of the Alps, and are evidence of links with other parts of Europe prior to the Roman invasion in AD 43.

Excavation of the findspot suggested that the hoard was buried in isolation on a small hill, perhaps as an offering to the gods.

The Winchester Hoard was acquired by the British Museum through the Treasure Act.

An example of a copper alloy *knotenfibeln* brooch from Aldermaston, West Berkshire. (HAMP-172E44)

36

16. Copper-alloy miniature wheel (HAMP-7A34A2)
Late Iron Age to Roman (100 BC–AD 100)
Found in North Waltham in 2016. Diameter 31.9 mm.

Finds of miniature objects (other than toys) turn up with relative frequency in most parts of Britain from the Bronze Age to Roman period. It is assumed that the purpose of their manufacture and deposition was mainly ritual. Miniature wheels, for instance, turn up at sites with sacred association across mainland Europe, as well as in southern and eastern Britain. This example, although undecorated, has a smooth and shiny surface patina. It has four spokes extending from a central cylinder to the curved inside edge of the felloe, the outside and upper and lower surfaces having been flattened-off.

It is likely that miniature wheels were associated with a sun god, and the discovery of one in a Norfolk hoard, found with a head of Jupiter, further supports this theory.

Late Iron Age/ Roman miniature wheel from North Waltham.

Examples of other Late Iron Age/ Roman miniature wheels of different designs and sizes recorded with the PAS. From left to right: SOM-E31AA6, WILT-D592A5 and WAW-360062.

17. Copper-alloy coin of the Suessiones (HAMP-F489F6)
Late Iron Age (120–50 BC)
Found in Crawley in 2015. Diameter 21.2 mm.

This cast coin, known as a *'potin'*, was made by the Suessiones tribe, who occupied the area of modern-day western Belgium and north-eastern France. It is known as the 'Confronted Goats' type after the image on one side of the coin; the opposite side shows a wolf and a boar. Continental coins of this date, although infrequent finds, are not unusual in Hampshire. A number of examples from other tribes in *Gallo Belgica* have been recorded on the database in recent years, and have also turned up as site finds, including a significant number during excavations at Calleva (Silchester). They are an important indicator of links with the Continent in the centuries before the Roman conquest.

Late Iron Age coin of the Suessiones from Crawley.

A Continental 'Champagne Wild Man' potin of the Senones of South Champagne and North Burgundy from Overton. (SUR-E40108)

Another coin of the Suessiones. This one was cut in half in antiquity and is from South Wonston. It is known as a 'Soissons Eye Boar' potin, because of the depiction of the reverse of a boar over an eye. (HAMP-39AE23)

18. Silver coin of Eppillus (HAMP-DE0DEA)
Late Iron Age (20 BC–AD 10)
Found in Dummer in 2014. Diameter 12.5 mm.

The Iron Age town or *oppidum* of Calleva at modern-day Silchester was a tribal centre of the Atrebates, ruled by Commios from about 50 BC. He was succeeded by his three sons, one of whom was Eppillus. This coin is a silver unit struck at Calleva, as can be seen from the inscription 'CALLE' on the obverse (head side). 'REX', Latin for 'king', is added to show an affinity with Rome. Another Roman symbol, the eagle, is depicted on the reverse with the inscription 'EPP', for Eppillus.

Most coins of Iron Age date are uninscribed and often feature abstract animals and heads. They tend to be regional in distribution, not travelling a great distance from their place of origin. The same is largely true of those that do have inscriptions but, due to the lettering, they can communicate much more to us about the different tribes and rulers at the time. Thanks to these inscriptions we know of two other mints in addition to that at Calleva. These are the mints at Camulodunum (Colchester, Essex) and Verulamium (St Albans, Hertfordshire).

Top left: Iron Age silver unit of Eppillus from Dummer.

Top right: An uninscribed, Chute-type gold stater from Ropley, with a stylised head on one side and horse on the other. These are thought to be based on coins of Philip II of Macedon, which date from the fourth century BC. (HAMP-C9DF53)

Above left: An inscribed gold stater of Cunobelin, minted at Camulodunum and found in Cambridgeshire. (CAM-CD5F58)

Above right: An inscribed silver unit of Tasciovanus, struck at Verulamium and found in Essex. (BH-A8D8F8)

19. Cremation burial with copper-alloy bowl and ceramic beakers (SUR-8EA776)
Late Iron Age (AD 1–50)
Found in Ropley in 2012. Diameter 148 mm.

Occasionally a finder will discover something below the plough soil that needs further archaeological investigation. Such was the case with this discovery during a metal detecting rally. An area was excavated around the initial find – a metal bowl, the rim of which had become detached from the base. Adjacent to it were cremated bones, while alongside were the remains of two ceramic beakers, their upper parts having been lost, possibly as the result of plough damage. Inside the bowl, now at an angle, were the remains of a carbonised material and cremated bone, suggesting this was the original depository for the cremation.

The rim of the bowl is decorated on both faces with a band of notching between a pair of grooved lines. The vessel has been lathe-turned and its rounded, shallow base is typical of vessels of this date from southern Britain. The find is now in the Hampshire Cultural Trust collections.

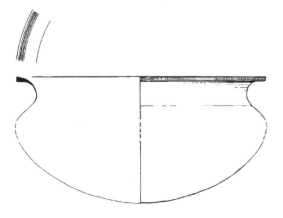

Above left: Excavation of the Late Iron Age cremation burial from Ropley.

Above right: Photograph detailing the separate base and (decorated) rim.

Left: Illustration of the bowl by David Williams.

Chapter 4
Roman Hampshire

The Roman period (AD 43–410) brings with it organisation and taxation. Coins minted from centres across the Roman Empire are prolific discoveries countywide – indeed, one in three finds recorded in Hampshire is a Roman coin. There is evidence of both large and small villas and farmsteads, particularly on the chalk downlands, and new smaller towns as well as the large civitas towns of Venta Belgarum and Calleva Atrebatum (Winchester and Silchester). Road systems connect these centres with places such as Londinium and Noviomagus (Chichester). We see fine mosaics in some of the larger villas (like Sparsholt, Fullerton and Thruxton), and an important temple site to Mars at Hayling Island. The introduction of pottery and salt-extraction industries also characterise the period, with the former famously in the New Forest and Alice Holt Forest but also in other locations across the county, and the latter at sites such as Warsash and Emsworth along the coast.

Much evidence of burial practice has been uncovered across the county. Excavations of an extensive cemetery site, Lankhills, to the north of Winchester indicate important links with Europe and, thanks to isotope analysis of skeletal remains, possibly even North Africa.

In the fourth century, forts (known as Saxon Shore Forts) were constructed along the south coast, two of which were in Hampshire, at Bitterne and Portchester, indicative of an ever-present Frankish and Saxon threat. Portchester, along with the Roman town walls and amphitheatre at Silchester, survive astonishingly well.

Finds associated with the Roman occupation are far more numerous than in previous periods and include often vast quantities of pottery vessels, coins, brooches, bracelets and other items of domestic, personal and military use.

A late Roman military buckle plate from Ropley. (HAMP-6636CF)

Top left: A stretch of the surviving town walls of Silchester, from the northern part of the circuit. (Katie Hinds)

Top right: A late Roman nail cleaner, often associated with the military. Found in Andover. (HAMP-E27943)

Above left: The fourth-century mosaic from Sparsholt villa, now in Winchester City Museum. (Winchester City Council; provided by Hampshire Cultural Trust)

Above right: A Roman 'trumpet' brooch, from Hursley and dating to the late first century/ early second century. (HAMP-4BDC1A)

20. Copper-alloy brooch (SUR-EA49AD)
Late Iron Age/Early Roman (40 BC–AD 100)
Found in Nether Wallop in 2015. Length 24.2 mm.

While brooches make an appearance in the archaeological record from around 400 BC, it is not until the later Iron Age and Roman periods that they become numerous. Flat animal brooches are not uncommon finds from the second century AD, but this example of a fully modelled hare brooch is rather more unusual. The animal has a rectangular head and grooved mouth, two bulbous eyes and a pair of conjoined ears, which slope at an angle away from the head. The back arches to a short tail, which is now incomplete. The legs are joined together in pairs, the front pair with a groove for the missing hinged pin and the rear pair retaining an edge of the missing catchplate. Both sides of the body are decorated with a line of punched crescents.

Above left: Late Iron Age/ Early Roman hare brooch from Nether Wallop.

Above right: A second-century AD plate brooch with enamel decoration depicting a hare, from the Isle of Wight. (IOW-50E085)

Below: The hare was a popular subject in the Roman period. This hound-chasing-a-hare knife handle from Old Alresford is a relatively common type. It is missing its iron blade, which would have folded beneath the handle when not in use. (HAMP-8C8E54)

21. Copper-alloy figurine (HAMP-378231)
Roman (AD 100–300)
Found in Andover in 2005. Length 33.9 mm.

This small anthropomorphic figurine in the form of a bound captive is one of around twenty found across the Roman Empire, and the most southerly to have been found in Britannia. These figurines seem to cluster in Britain and on the Rhine/Danube frontier, although only a few have been found in dateable archaeological contexts. It is likely that they are a representation of a slave. The head has a distinctively 'Celtic' tonsure with the hair brushed back from the forehead and shaved behind the crown. A rope loops around neck, hands and feet. The figurine is solid with two perforations, horizontally and vertically aligned. Clearly the figurine was intended to be mounted, but who was meant to see it and for what purpose it was made are less clear.

Above left: A Roman bound-captive figurine from Andover.

Above right: The line drawing of the figurine depicts the detail clearly. (Illustration by Alan Cracknell)

Left: The amphitheatre at Silchester. Although there is no surviving evidence to suggest what took place in the arena, it is not inconceivable to imagine bound captives there, perhaps as part of a gladiatorial spectacle. (Katie Hinds)

22. Gold coin of Septimius Severus (HAMP-474144)
Roman (AD 202–10)
Found in Crondall in 2015. Diameter 14.7 mm.

Roman coins are the mostly frequently recorded artefact on the PAS database, with those of the third and fourth centuries being most common. At peak production, millions of these coins must have been produced per day. While Roman silver coins are less common than those of copper alloy, far more scarce are those made of gold. Only seven are currently recorded from Hampshire on the PAS database, including this example of a *quinarius* of Septimius Severus, who ruled from AD 193 to 211. On the obverse (head side) is a laureate head facing right with the inscription SEVERVS PIVS AVG. The reverse depicts a Victory advancing left, holding wreath and palm, with the legend COS III PP (third consulship, Pater Patriae – 'father of his country'). Minted in Rome, this coin has only been recorded before in silver.

The *quinarius* would have been worth half an *aureus*, roughly two weeks' pay for a legionary soldier.

Roman gold *quinarius* of Septimius Severus from Crondall.

An earlier Roman gold coin, the *aureus*. This was struck in the first century AD during the reign of Claudius; it was found in Odiham. (BUC-1A1EFF)

23. Ceramic indented beaker (HAMP-0C24F1)
Roman (AD 240–400)
Found in Hyde (New Forest) in the 1950s. Height 180 mm.

Fine colour-coated tableware produced in the New Forest kilns in the late third and fourth century are found all across the south of England. Although not heavily populated at this time, a rich industry grew up in the area supplying coarse as well as fine wares. One of the busiest areas was at Sloden Inclosure, where this indented beaker was found (a distinctive New Forest type). It has been repaired since its discovery. The slip is patchy and of varying colour, suggesting that the beaker might have been a 'waster' (damaged during production and so discarded). The base has a beaded rim and underneath is a spiral, a product of being wheel-thrown.

Indented beakers come in many sizes, and specialists theorise that the larger might have been used for drinking beer, while the smaller were for wine, although there is no evidence to support this!

Left: A Roman indented beaker from Hyde.

Right above: New Forest Ware vessels from Rockbourne Roman villa. (Hampshire County Council; provided by Hampshire Cultural Trust)

Right below: Roman pottery kiln reconstruction at Montans archeosite museum, France. (Magerius via Wikimedia Commons)

24. Silver coin of Constantine II (HAMP-2197A7)
Roman (AD 337–40)
Found in Hurstbourne Priors in 2009. Diameter 26.2 mm

The *miliarensis* was introduced as a denomination during the reign of Constantine I. Its value was one thousandth of a pound of gold, and they are unusual finds, often surviving only fragmentarily due to their thinness. This example is a rare coin, struck during the reign of Constantine II at the mint of Thessalonica in eastern Greece (indicated by the letters TES on the reverse of the coin). On the obverse the bust faces right, wearing drapery and a cuirass (armour). The inscription reads: FL CL CONSTANTINVS P F AVG (son of Constantine, pious and felix, Augustus). On the reverse is a soldier in military dress holding a spear and resting on a shield. The inscription reads: VIRTVS EXERCITVS (the valour of the Roman army). The British Museum has an example struck from different dies. What is particularly interesting about this coin, however, is that it was issued so late in Constantine II's reign; perhaps it was struck after his assassination (in AD 340) but before the mint of Thessalonica could be notified of his death.

A silver Roman *miliarensis* of Constantine II from Hurstbourne Priors.

A rather more typical find, a late third-century radiate (so-called because of the spikey crown the emperor is wearing) of Carausius from Dummer. (HAMP-DE5FF3)

Another more frequent coin type, a fourth-century *nummus* of Constantius II from Wiltshire, commemorating the glory of the Roman army. (HAMP-263903)

25. Copper-alloy figurine (HAMP-8703D7)
Roman (AD 43–410)
Found in Crondall in 2015. Length 26.2 mm.

Miniature representations were popular in the Roman period and are often related to a cult of some kind, with divine figurines and their familiars being especially common. The relative frequency of such discoveries supports the idea that portable shrines were probably commonplace within the Romano-British household.

This rather characterful bearded goat figurine stands with his head turned away from his body. His long triangular beard is decorated with moulded vertical lines to represent his hair, as is the body. The curving horns are damaged and both feet are missing.

The goat is thought to be a dedication to Mercury, the messenger god, who is often depicted with a winged hat and winged shoes. Mercury is associated with wealth and commerce, as well as guiding souls to the underworld.

Above left: A Roman goat figurine from Crondall.

Above right: Another Hampshire goat from Popham, illustration by Alan Cracknell. (HAMP2606)

Left: A figurine of Mercury's head, identifiable by his winged hat, from Wiltshire. (HAMP-511229)

26. Gold finger ring (HAMP-EC91E2)
Roman (AD 300–400)
Found in Tangley in 2014. Diameter 22.3 mm.

As with gold coinage, objects made from this precious metal are rare finds. This ring, unfortunately discovered damaged, has fine gold filigree decoration around the shoulders and is set with an intaglio made of a derivative of onyx known as nicolo. The nicolo is engraved with a naked adolescent leaning on a column and holding a flaming torch. Wings sprout from his shoulders to show he is a depiction of Cupid, the god of love and desire.

It is tempting to think of this as a betrothal ring but Cupid was also capable of doing much mischief with his bow and arrow. This ring was acquired by Hampshire Cultural Trust through the Treasure Act.

Above left: A Roman gold and gemstone finger ring from Tangley.

Above right: An unusual Roman finger ring from Wiltshire, formed from a section of bracelet and presumably reused once the bracelet had broken. (HAMP-9453AE)

Below: Examples of more common Roman finger-ring types (made of copper alloy) that have been recorded with PAS.

27. Copper-alloy spatula handle (HAMP3507)
Roman (AD 100–250)
Found in Micheldever in 2001. Length 51 mm.

When the Romans invaded Britannia in AD 43, they brought with them many things that were new and different, with fashions, coinage and lifestyle choices among them. With this would have come literacy, suggested by discoveries of writing equipment such as styli, wax tablets and wax spatulas. The Portable Antiquities Scheme has recorded examples of the latter from central, eastern and northern Britain, and there are now five recorded from Hampshire, including this example. It depicts the bust of Minerva, goddess of wisdom and learning, with wavy hair and a high Corinthian helmet. The facial features are worn, but the hair is picked out with incised lines. Minerva wears one of her attributes – the *aegis* – over the upper body: a shield or animal skin with a Gorgon's mask at the centre. The object in her left hand is unidentifiable. The area below has a slot to take the missing iron blade – this would have been used to smooth out the wax on a tablet so that it could be reused.

There are now over forty examples of Minerva spatula handles on the PAS database, with further wax spatula handles of plainer form, providing important evidence for the extent of literacy in Roman Britain. There were thought to be only eight spatula handles prior to the inception of the Portable Antiquities Scheme with another twenty or so known from the Low Countries, France and Germany. Metal detectorists who record their finds and add to the record can transform our understanding of the past.

In addition to the five PAS examples from Hampshire, there is also one from excavations at Silchester.

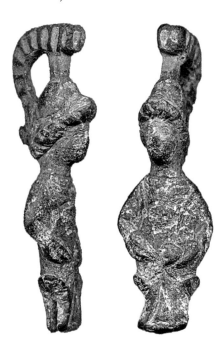

Roman Minerva spatula handle from Micheldever.

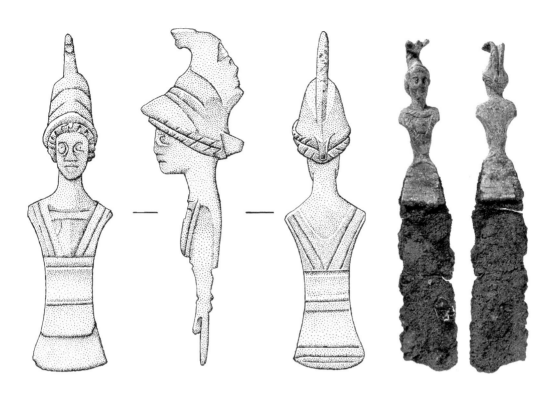

Above left: A line drawing of another Minerva spatula handle from Odiham, by Alan Cracknell. (HAMP-4EB6C5)

Above right: A Roman Minerva spatula with much of the blade remaining, from Wiltshire. (WILT-9ECD01)

Below: A stylus with spatulate terminal – a Roman pencil/eraser combination – from Wiltshire. (WILT-70D3C3)

Chapter 5
Saxon Hampshire

After the decline of the Roman Empire, we see the introduction of smaller Anglo-Saxon farmsteads, villages and communities, and a landscape we would recognise today. During the transition period, the earliest Anglo-Saxon graves still produce some Roman grave goods, but later we see the building of churches (for example at Breamore and Boarhunt) and the establishment of the kingdom of Wessex.

During the early Saxon period, our evidence comes from settlements (again focused on the chalk downlands and the river valleys) and many cemeteries (including some of mixed-rite cremation and burial at Itchen Abbas, Worthy Park and Portway, Andover). The finds from this period are not common and include varied brooch types such as the button brooch and saucer brooch, buckles, dress hooks and other personal items often decorated in a zoomorphic style (with animal representation), and silver and gold coinage. There are stylistic variations in design at this time, reflecting the different Germanic peoples who settled here. These were mostly Saxons, but the Meonwara (those living along the Meon Valley) and those in the Solent region and Isle of Wight were Jutes.

In the middle of this period Winchester and Hamwic (Southampton) were established as trade centres, and Romsey developed as an ecclesiastical centre. Southampton in particular has been extensively excavated and much of the town's external boundary has been discovered, while the Saxon settlement at Winchester lies beneath the medieval and present city. During the later period we see the growth of these settlements, Winchester becoming an important ecclesiastical centre; while there must have been a threat from Viking raids, this is visible only in occasional finds of Scandinavian origin. Other finds from the period include silver pennies, decorative personal ornaments (usually with an animal design) and, in the eleventh century in particular, numerous fittings associated with horses.

Annular and saucer brooches of the late fifth/early sixth centuries, from excavations at Mount Pleasant, Alton. (Hampshire County Council; provided by Hampshire Cultural Trust)

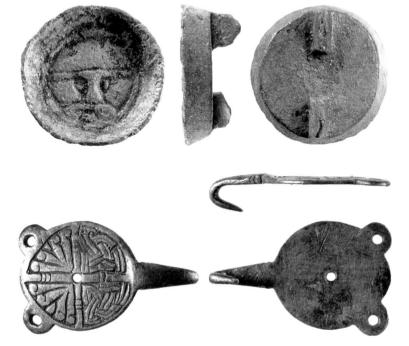

Button brooch of the late fifth/early sixth century, depicting a helmeted human face at the centre, from Soberton. (HAMP-914D62)

A ninth-century silver dress hook with lobed Trewhiddle-style plant tendrils and double-strand interlace, from Andover. (HAMP-0B4001)

28. Copper-alloy and enamel mount (HAMP-FFCDF4)
Early Anglo-Saxon (AD 450–550)
Found in St Mary Bourne in 2013. Diameter 78.4 mm.

This enigmatic object is a near-complete furniture or strap mount, decorated on one face only. At the centre is a rivet hole with traces of orange staining, suggesting that the lost rivet was made of iron. Surrounding this is a hexagon of six triangles on a red enamel background. Beyond are three pairs of confronted animals with their heads turned backwards, biting their tails. Around the external rim is a border of 'O' and 'X' shapes, set above a second border of triangles.

No parallel has been found for the decoration. The back-turned animals with tails in their mouths are seen in the 'Quoit Brooch Style', which dates to the mid-fifth century, with its distribution extending into northern France. These animals are also seen, differently executed, on a vessel from northern Gaul that dates to the late fifth or early sixth century. However, enamel decoration, the use of geometric patterning and a vandyked border (of conjoined triangles) is unknown from Anglo-Saxon period, and may suggest a Roman or Celtic influence. This raises interesting questions about what Hampshire's links were with the wider world after the fall of the Roman Empire and its subsequent withdrawal from Britain.

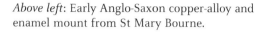

Above left: Early Anglo-Saxon copper-alloy and enamel mount from St Mary Bourne.

Above right: The Roman Ilam pan from the Staffordshire Moorlands, which is inscribed with the name of four forts along Hadrian's Wall. It has vandyked decoration. (WMID-3FE965)

Left: A scabbard mount from Cheriton, decorated in the Quoit Brooch Style. (SUR-029B13)

29. Copper-alloy bucket (FASW-93BE6C)
Early Anglo-Saxon (AD 500–600)
Found in Breamore in 1999.

One of a small group of eleven known examples, with only two others being from Britain, is this extraordinary find of a bucket with a Greek inscription around the rim and a detailed hunting scene, depicting three warriors confronting a fierce leopard and a hyena or bear. The body of the bucket was produced from a single sheet of metal, the decoration and inscription applied with a punch. Translated, the inscription reads, 'Use this in good health, lady, for many happy years', the inference of health suggesting that the bucket may have been used in a bathing context – several of the other buckets have similar inscriptions.

In terms of art history, the Breamore bucket is seen as a significant piece of Byzantine workmanship and can be paralleled with hunting scenes portrayed on mosaic pavements, particularly in Antioch (in modern-day Turkey). It is likely that all of the eleven known buckets were produced here, perhaps in the same workshop.

Thanks to the quick and responsible actions of the metal detectorist who found the Breamore bucket, archaeological investigation of the site followed, revealing a small Anglo-Saxon cemetery. This work was followed by a *Time Team Live* excavation in 2001, resulting in six burials and another six buckets, though these were copper-alloy wood-staved buckets and not Byzantine in origin. Interestingly, the Breamore bucket was not the only imported find at the cemetery – other finds include a glass bowl, likely imported from Cologne or north-east France/Belgium, and a Frankish buckle. The burials also contained an unprecedented number of spears and shields, but perhaps most unusual was the discovery of the practice of multiple burials within a single grave, which seems to have been the norm at Breamore but is only seen occasionally in other cemeteries of the same date.

Above: Illustration of the frieze on the Breamore bucket, detailing the scene and the handle; in this depiction the inscription begins with the last letter. (Illustration by Alan Cracknell)

Right: Early Anglo-Saxon Byzantine bucket from Breamore. (Hampshire Cultural Trust)

30. Copper-alloy mount (HAMP2432)
Early Anglo-Saxon (AD 600–650)
Found in Soberton in 2002. Length 30 mm.

The cult of Woden, the leading Anglo-Saxon and Germanic god, appears to have been established in southern England by at least the seventh century. Woden is recognisable through place names such as 'Wednesbury' in the West Midlands and 'Wansdyke' in Wiltshire and Somerset. Not much is known about him, but we do know that as a deity he was a mythical ancestor of Anglo-Saxon kings and that he is probably connected to the Norse god Odin.

This unusual and interesting object depicts the head of a bearded male wearing a horned helmet (forming the ring) with two close-set perforations for eyes. He has a vertical nose and two triangular cheeks. The lower half of the head has mouldings that represent the beard. Given its small size, it is likely this was a strap or clothing mount.

Horn-helmeted figures are known in Germanic areas from the seventh century to the early Viking period, but usually represent a whole person and not just a head. These are often shown in pairs, performing ceremonial dances with weapons, and it is thought that these are connected with the cult of Woden. Since this discovery, another three have been discovered, in Norfolk (two) and the East Riding of Yorkshire. Excavated, datable parallels include an embossed figure on an object from Sutton Hoo, which suggests a date in the first half of the seventh century. In 2013, an object of uncertain type, depicting a head with a horned helmet, was discovered in Crawley, Hampshire. Its closest parallel is the Soberton mount.

The object has been acquired by Hampshire Cultural Trust.

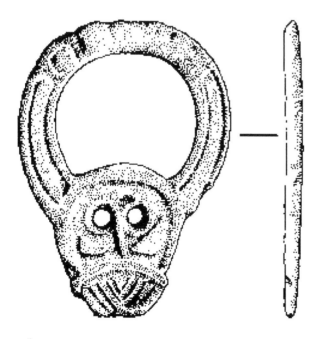

Illustration of the Soberton mount, by Alan Cracknell.

Anglo-Saxon mount depicting a horn-helmeted head from Soberton.

A possible die stamp of Early Anglo-Saxon date featuring a horn-helmeted figure, from Crawley. Length 31.3 mm. (HAMP-B292C2)

31. Copper-alloy, gilt and glass brooch (HAMP-9B6151)
Early Anglo-Saxon (AD 525–600)
Found in Wonston in 2007. Diameter 32.7 mm.

The variety of Continental influences we see in the Early Anglo-Saxon period are reflected in object design and decoration. There is great variety in brooch style and regional differences can be discerned. Many of those we know about are excavated cemetery finds, but metal detectorists are discovering similar finds on non-grave sites, showing that they were part of daily wear.

This gilded brooch has four triangular settings, filled with the remains of red glass (or possibly poor-quality garnet) around a circular area, which has traces of a white paste. In between the triangles is decoration of probable animal heads formed through a process known as chip-carving, where a wax or wood model is carved and used to create a mould for the intended object. Orange iron corrosion to the reverse of the object is from the missing pin.

This brooch is extremely similar in design to a type of brooch from Kent known as a keystone garnet brooch. These are made of gilded silver, inlaid with garnets. Behind the garnets is gold corrugated foil, the ridges of which reflect the light in different directions and give extra sparkle to the glass or garnet. What is interesting about this find is that it is clearly a cheap imitation, and we know of several others from Hampshire, Wiltshire, Berkshire and Oxfordshire, suggesting that there may well have been a local workshop making these more affordable versions. Although much of the gilding has now been lost, the surface would have originally been covered. Combined with the red glass, this brooch would have looked rather splendid when new.

Copper-alloy, gilt and glass brooch from Wonston.

A silver gilt Kentish keystone garnet brooch discovered on the Isle of Wight; note the corrugated foil behind the garnets. (IOW-A33D42)

58

32. Copper-alloy strap-end (HAMP-9E6A09)
Carolingian (AD 875–1000)
Found in Buriton in 2015. Length 27.6 mm.

An object type that first comes to our attention in the late Roman period is the strap-end, used predominantly by soldiers as part of their military dress. In the mid-to-late Anglo-Saxon period, strap-ends sometimes appear in precious metal with inlay and elaborate animal decoration but are more often made from copper alloy. These strap-ends almost always have their decoration vertically aligned, suggesting the straps were tied in knots and the ends left to hang downwards.

This strap-end is unusual in its shape and decoration. It is apparently complete, straight-sided and with a thin attachment plate at one end. The geometric decoration is symmetrical and consists of a central stem with extensions to either side. Two rivets remain intact for attaching to a strap. It is thought this type probably derives from spur straps.

The vegetal 'stem' decoration suggests that the object is Carolingian in origin. At this time there were connections between the Carolingian continent (present-day France and Belgium) and the kingdom of Wessex, of which Hampshire was at the heart. However it may have come here with the Vikings, following their Continental raids in the ninth and tenth century. A very similar object is known from Norfolk.

A Carolingian
strap-end from
Buriton.

Another Hampshire find of Carolingian style – a mount from Micheldever with vegetal, 'vine leaf' decoration, silver inlay and gilding. (HAMP-F22C4B)

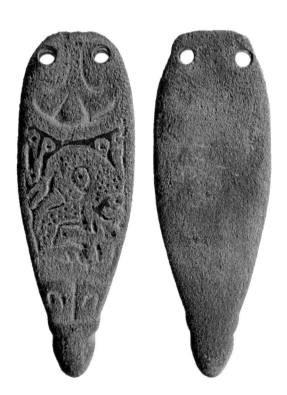

Of similar date but a very different style is this Anglo Saxon strap-end, typical of those found in south-east England. (HAMP-455B11)

33. Silver coin of Eadgar (HAMP-C4B478)
Late Anglo-Saxon (AD 959–973)
Found in St Mary Bourne in 2011. Diameter 21.2 mm.

During the eighth century, the first of the broad, thin silver coins that we know as pennies appear and remain the main form of currency in England for the next 500 years (see additional images below). In 973, King Eadgar the Peaceful standardised the coinage and, from this time, the king's portrait and name appear on the obverse (the head side) while a cross with the mint name (and moneyer in the earlier periods) are seen on the reverse. This coin dates to the period leading up to the reform phase, between 959 and 973. These earlier coins often include portraits, but also monograms and various cross designs. This particular coin is of the 'circumscription cross' type and depicts a small cross at the centre of both faces. On the obverse the king's name is inscribed around the edge, starting from the initial mark (a cross) aligned at 12 o'clock: EADGAR REX TO BR-I (Eadgar, king of all Britain). The reverse is particularly interesting. It reads: LEOIRIC MO VVINCI (Leofric, moneyer at Winchester). This is the first of this type of coin with Leofric as moneyer at Winchester. While he is noted to have minted coins in the reign of Athelstan (924–39), he is not known to have struck coins of the intervening kings. Could it be the same man, or perhaps his son? Unfortunately we can only speculate.

A silver penny of Eadgar from St Mary Bourne.

A silver penny of Aethelstan I of East Anglia, dating to *c.* 827 and from Chilbolton. (HAMP-822403)

Examples of pennies during the medieval period: A silver penny of John, dating to 1204/5. 'Short cross' pennies such as this one were issued during the reigns of Henry II, Richard I, John and Henry III, and all bear the obverse legend HENRICVS REX. (HAMP-45744E)

A silver penny of Edward I, dating to 1279, found in West Sussex. (HAMP-3B4545)

34. Silver gilt coin brooch (WILT-C94353)
Late Anglo-Saxon (AD 1050–3)
Found in Nether Wallop in 2013. Diameter 19.1 mm.

The contemporaneous reuse of artefacts is always of particular interest – why did they do this? Had the original artefact become useless in its current form? If not, what was gained by changing it?

During the middle of the eleventh century, mainly in the reigns of Edward the Confessor and William I, we see an unusual phenomenon – modified silver pennies issued between 1050 and 1075, reused as a brooch or badge. The pin fittings are usually added to the obverse (head) side of the coin, while the reverse is usually gilded. At this period the reverse design is often a cross, suggesting a reference to Christianity. The PAS has recorded twenty-five of these finds from central and southern England. Given their rather flimsy nature, they can perhaps be regarded as functioning as a badge rather than a brooch. Their wider purpose, however, is more elusive – perhaps they simply reflect a particular fashion at the time.

This example is missing its pin but retains the brooch attachments in the form of two strips of metal held in place by rivets. The gilded reverse is of the 'Expanding Cross' type (the most common of the coin brooches), depicting a small cross with the legend GODESBRAND ON SCRE. On the obverse is a helmeted bust holding a sceptre, with the legend EDPERD [REX]. This is a coin of Edward the Confessor, struck at the mint in Shrewsbury by Godesbrand between 1050 and 1053. It is only the second of its type recorded with this moneyer.

The brooch was acquired by the British Museum after being declared Treasure.

A silver gilt coin brooch from Nether Wallop.

A silver gilt William I coin brooch, missing its fittings and pin. It is from Micheldever and was acquired by Hampshire Cultural Trust through the Treasure Act. (HAMP-6CAD57)

35. Copper-alloy stirrup-strap mount (HAMP-9DA925)
Late Anglo-Saxon/Early Norman (AD 1070–1140)
Found in Cheriton in 2014. Length 51.5 mm.

The importance of the horse as a means of travel in antiquity is often reflected in finds, be it with representations of the horse on decorations or with objects that would have adorned it. This object is a stirrup-strap mount, which would have been positioned at the apex of the stirrup and attached to a strap suspended from the saddle. They are thought to date to the eleventh century and often feature Anglo-Scandinavian decoration. This example, however, is thought to reflect Norman Romanesque art styles and so it is dated slightly later.

The mount is triangular in shape and depicts in high relief a right-facing lion standing on three legs, the remaining forepaw raised upwards and the tail curling up over the back. The head tips backwards with open jaws, and above this is a moulded diamond. The neck is decorated in imitation of a mane. A border flanks the edge of the object with a tri-lobed terminal above the diamond; this retains traces of an iron rivet for attachment to the strap. The reverse of the object has remains of two further iron rivets, for attachment to the stirrup.

This type is the most common of the stirrup-strap mounts and the lion can face either right or left.

A Late Anglo-Saxon/Early Norman stirrup-strap mount from Cheriton.

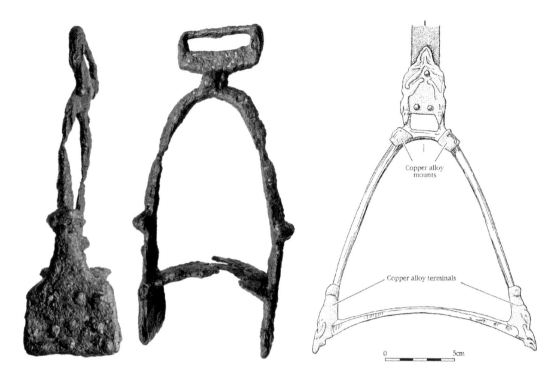

Above left: A complete eleventh-century iron probable Viking stirrup from Warwickshire. (WAW-989551)

Above right: An iron stirrup from Chalgrove, Oxfordshire, with copper-alloy terminals and collars. A strap-mount is shown in position. (David Williams)

Below: A zoomorphic stirrup terminal of eleventh-century date from Wiltshire, depicting an animal's head with bulging elongated eyes and a prominent snout, with a pronounced lip to the front. Length 32.8 mm. (HAMP-593565)

Chapter 6
Medieval Hampshire

The medieval period (1066–1500 AD) sees the cities of Winchester and Southampton expand. The St Giles Fair, to the east of Winchester, and Southampton's port status contribute to increased trade between Hampshire and the Continent. Both centres retain parts of their defensive walls and gates. We also see the development of new towns such as New Alresford, Stockbridge and Newtown. Other physical evidence from the medieval period can be seen in motte or ring-and-bailey castles (Barley Pound, Crondall, for example), ridge-and-furrow remains of agricultural practices and deserted medieval villages (such as those at Abbotstone, Popham and Foxcotte). Bishop's Waltham Palace and Wolvesey Castle are more substantial stone structures, built for visiting royalty and the bishops of Winchester. The Church, in particular, expanded during this period and we see monastic foundations across Hampshire, such as Netley Abbey and Beaulieu Abbey.

A medieval iron forked arrowhead, probably for hunting, from Hursley. (HAMP-39EFDA)

Above left: The deserted medieval village of Abbotstone, which declined with the growth of nearby Alresford, looking south-west. (Katie Hinds)

Above right: Abbotstone deserted medieval village, looking north-east. (Katie Hinds)

Below: A lead papal bulla of Pope Clement VI (1342–52), which would have sealed a missive from Rome. St Peter and St Paul are depicted on the obverse. These are often discovered close to the religious establishments to which they would have been sent. Found in Wherwell. (HAMP-A295D7)

The finds of the medieval period reflect these changes – silver pennies (cut to make halfpennies and farthings) are typical discoveries, as are dress and household accessories and implements. The church too is reflected in many finds, for example in no. 36 below. Hunting tools are occasionally brought in for recording, a reminder of the numerous royal forests at this time (of which the New Forest is one). These were popular for hunting but only for use by the aristocracy.

36. Copper-alloy cross (HAMP-A33213)
Medieval (AD 1175–1300)
Found in Bishop's Waltham in 2009. Length 54.2 mm.

The city of Limoges in west-central France was the centre of enamel production in Europe during the earlier medieval period. Limoges produced beautifully coloured works of art, in the form of crucifixes, reliquaries and mounts of various kinds. These were affordable by the wealthy but most parish churches would probably have had a Limoges enamel cross for the altar. Although not common finds, discoveries of Limoges enamel plaques turn up occasionally, as do figures from reliquary caskets. The plaques are often from a processional or altar cross, and feature symbols for the four evangelists – saints Matthew, Mark, Luke and John – at each of the cardinal points.

This object is a little damaged but is a plaque from a crucifix, depicting a winged and haloed man in low relief: St Matthew as an angel representing the incarnation of Jesus. Above the halo is a small cross. Although no enamel survives, it would have originally filled the recessed areas, probably in blues, reds, whites and greens. The raised areas around the enamel would have been gilded, creating quite a sight, especially in the candlelight of a church or chapel.

Medieval Limoges cross mount from Bishop's Waltham.

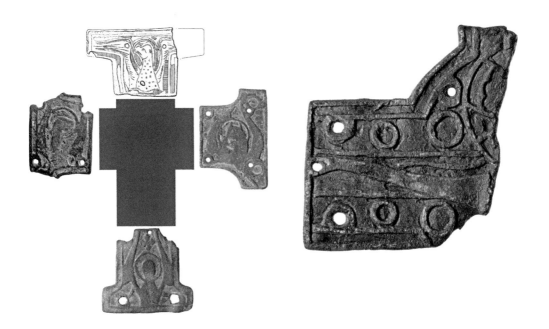

Above left: Author's recreation of a Limoges cross, featuring (clockwise from top) the eagle of St John (NMS-0241D8), the ox of St Luke (SUSS-54B2C4), St Matthew as an angel (HAMP-A33213) and the lion of St Mark (BERK-B1ADDB). All are depicted winged and haloed.

Above right: From the centre of a crucifix, this is a fragment of Limoges plaque featuring Christ on the cross. From Suffolk. (SF-980602)

Below: A representation of a saint or apostle from a reliquary casket – another product of the Limoges industry. From Devon. (DEV-F8EC7C)

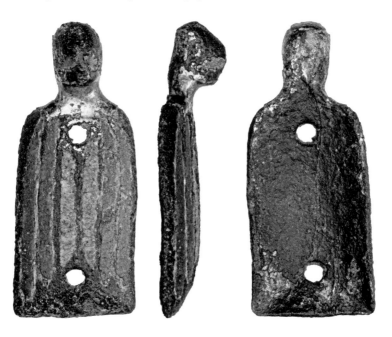

37. Copper-alloy matrix (SUR-AB43CB)
Medieval (AD 1300–1500)
Found in Buriton in 2015. Diameter 11.1 mm.

From the late medieval period until the nineteenth century, cloth seals were used to authenticate pieces of cloth that had been produced to a recognised standard. An authenticator called an alnager would have enforced this. The seals were made of lead or wax.

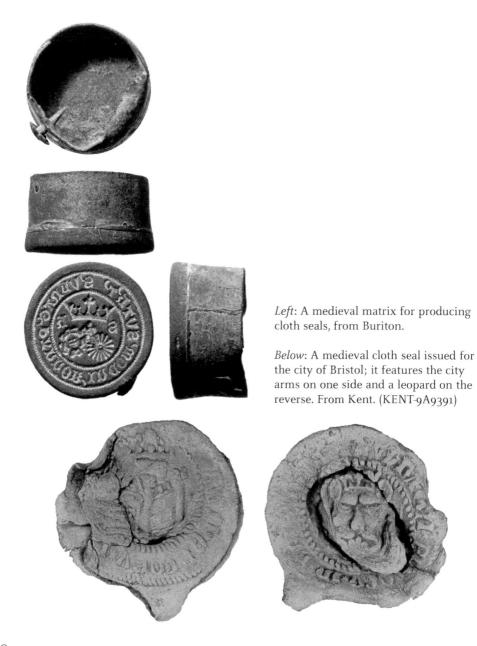

Left: A medieval matrix for producing cloth seals, from Buriton.

Below: A medieval cloth seal issued for the city of Bristol; it features the city arms on one side and a leopard on the reverse. From Kent. (KENT-9A9391)

This object is a matrix for producing cloth seals. While cloth seals are relatively common finds, the matrices to produce them are not. This matrix is circular, with a collar soldered to it and a rivet at the side join. It would originally have had a handle, probably of wood. The depiction on the matrix is of a crown above a rose, a fleur-de-lis, and a possible spur rowel. The letters 'S H' appear to either side and the legend around reads S'VLNAG PANNOR' IN COM' SVTH 'T', which is Latin for 'Seal of Ulnage for Cloth in the County of Southampton'. The S H may simply stand for Southampton.

Unfortunately no cloth seal is known with this design, which suggests the resulting cloth seals may have been made of wax. Indeed, lead seals from this period are scarce compared to those a couple of centuries later. In addition, the Parliamentary Rolls of medieval England suggest that steel is used for the production of lead cloth-seal matrices. However, we do know of cloth seals with a similar design and of one other Southampton matrix with a similar inscription, suggesting that this example dates to the late fourteenth or early fifteenth century.

38. Gold and garnet pendant (HAMP-53CCA3)
Late Medieval (AD 1400–1500)
Found in Sherfield English in 2014. Length 24.2 mm.

This beautiful object would almost certainly have been worn by a member of the nobility or someone of great wealth, probably for a formal occasion and as part of a larger ensemble of jewellery. It is a pendant comprising three parts, two of which are thin sheet gold in the form of five double petals. The lower petals are decorated with hammered decoration (and incised radiating lines to the reverse), and the upper with grooved zig-zag lines. These two parts are stacked below the third, which is a cabochon (rounded and polished) almandine garnet gemstone. This is set in a claw bezel, from which a rivet protrudes from the reverse and penetrates the two sheet plates to secure the group together. At the top of the pendant is a soldered gold wire loop for suspension. At the opposite end of the pendant are three smaller loops. It is likely that these would have carried short chains for another attachment, possibly a pearl. The most famous comparable example is a pendant in the Fishpool Hoard from Nottinghamshire, which dates no later than 1464.

Analysis of the surface of the metal by the British Museum noted a point of interest: the surface composition for the main body of the pendant (the petals) and the suspension loop was approximately 83–85 per cent gold (the remainder being silver and copper alloy). The claw setting and rivet are slightly less at 70–74 per cent gold, suggesting the parts were not made together.

The find was declared Treasure under the Treasure Act.

A fifteenth-century gold and garnet pendant from Sherfield English.

A medieval gold pendant, with short chains and set with an amethyst, from Lincolnshire. (DENO-65C775)

A gold and garnet chain link from a necklace, decorated with sixteen small pearls. It is of similar construction to the Sherfield English find. From Lincolnshire. (LIN-095207)

Ampullae are miniature flasks containing holy water that would have been touted as souvenirs to those on pilgrimage. They usually have a loop on either side for suspension, and it is likely that they were worn around the neck to keep the precious water close to the heart. Pilgrimage played a big part in many people's lives and, apart from the large, well-known destinations such as Canterbury (for St Thomas Becket) and Walsingham (the Blessed Virgin Mary), there were many smaller pilgrimage sites around the country.

This particular example was discovered by someone digging their garden. The rounded end depicts a scallop shell (the symbol of pilgrimage) on one side while the neck above depicts a possible representation of the mitred head of St Thomas Becket, perhaps beneath a canopy. The other face shows a five-petalled flower within a raised circle. Between this and the decorated curving edge is a raised cross fourchée. The open end of the neck would have been crimped shut, to seal in the holy water.

The popularity of *ampullae* started to wane with the introduction of the pilgrim badge in the early fourteenth century, although it is thought that they continued in use to the end of the fifteenth century. The violent murder in 1170 of Thomas Becket, Archbishop of Canterbury, sent shockwaves through the Christian world. A resulting cult, and Becket's canonisation by Pope Alexander III, meant that Canterbury soon became a major destination for pilgrims.

Medieval lead ampulla from Overton.

A pilgrim badge, depicting the bust of Thomas Becket. (NMGW-DB8D66)

An ornate medieval pilgrim badge, depicting the martyrdom of Thomas Becket, from Greater London. (PUBLIC-364487)

An illustration by Alan Cracknell of a lead *ampulla* from Soberton with a crowned 'W' to one side and a scallop shell on the other. The 'W' is seen frequently on *ampullae* and is thought to refer to the cult of Our Lady of Walsingham in Norfolk. (HAMP1810)

40. Copper-alloy jetton (HAMP-9F4197)
Late Medieval (AD 1461–97)
Found in Hursley in 2013. Diameter 25 mm.

A *jetton*, so-named after the French verb *jeter,* meaning 'to throw', was used as part of an accounting system on chequered cloth, similar in application to an abacus. Many jettons were produced in the later medieval and post-medieval periods, and it is thought that they probably had secondary uses – for example, as gaming counters. They are coin-like in their appearance, though always made of base metal. While some of the earlier English issues depict the king's bust on one side, as time goes on the design becomes quite varied.

This example is of French origin (these tend to dominate the later medieval jetton market), struck at Tournai. It is the principal design under the reigns of Louis XI (1461–83) and Charles VIII (1483–97), the fleur-de-lis being symbolic of the Royal Arms of France on which it appears. This face of the jetton has the accompanying inscription VIVE LE ROI VIVE LE ROI VIE, 'long live the king'. The reverse of the jetton shows a cross pattée, surrounded by sprigs and the inscription GETTES BIEN PAIES BIEN, which appears to translate as 'cast well, pay well' – if your jetton sums are right, then you will pay the correct amount.

Late medieval Tournai jetton from Hursley.

An early fourteenth-century English jetton found in a Winchester garden, featuring the same bust as pennies of the time. English jettons were gradually superseded in popularity by those from France and the Low Countries. (HAMP-6483E6)

A later seventeenth-century jetton struck at Nuremberg by Hans Schultes III. Nuremberg jettons dominate the market in the post-medieval period. (HAMP-A5CBA8)

41. Gold coins of Henry VI and Henry VII (HAMP-31E154 and HAMP-FEE0E5)
Late Medieval (deposited after AD 1488/9)
Found near Andover in 2010 and 2011. Diameters 29.1 mm and 27.5 mm.

Although found 20 metres apart, these coins are far too unusual to be single losses; rather, it is likely that they constitute a purse drop. Both coins are *angels*, a denomination so-called because of the depiction of St Michael the Archangel spearing the dragon on the obverse, in place of the usual portrait of the king. This change of design befits a time when knightly pursuits and pious deeds were popular with the public. Alternatively, the *angel* could have a more spiritual significance and the coins may have been deposited intentionally for a reason now lost to us.

The *angel* of Henry VI was minted at Bristol (denoted by the B in the depiction of the sea on the reverse) between 1470 and 1471. The *angel* of Henry VII was minted at the Tower of London between 1488 and 1489. However, this latter coin has been clipped at the edges, suggesting that it would have circulated for a while after its issue; consequently, it is likely that the coins were lost or deposited sometime afterwards. The coins are comparable to those in the Asthall hoard (Oxfordshire), which might have been buried as late as the 1520s.

Both coins have a similar obverse legend, which translates as 'Henry, by the grace of God, King of England and France, Lord'. The reverses are also similar and continue the religious overtone, depicting a ship with a large cross as the mast from which the royal shield is hanging.

The Henry VI reverse reads PER CRVCE' TVA SALVA nOS XPC REDE'TOR ('Through thy cross save us, Christ Redeemer'), while the Henry VII reverse reads IhC AVTE TRAnSIEnS PER mEDIV ILORV ('Jesus passing through their midst went His way').

The *angel* was worth six shillings and sixpence (in the region of £145 in present-day currency).

Gold *angel* of Henry VI, minted at Bristol, from near Andover.

Gold *angel* of Henry VII, minted at the Tower of London, from near Andover.

An earlier gold coin from the previous century, a *half noble* of Edward III, struck at London between 1363 and 1369. This is from a coin hoard discovered in Upton Grey. (HAMP-6226E8)

42. Copper-alloy gilt book fitting (HAMP-C0F9E7)
Medieval (AD 1350–1500)
Found in Hawkley in 2010. Length 44.7 mm.

This object consists of two hollow parts, with one rectangular and one diamond-shaped section, and an animal terminal, perhaps representing a dragon. The rectangular section has a rivet hole at the open end for securing to a strap, while the diamond-shaped element has a central hole on its underside. Both retain traces of the gilding that would have originally covered the entire surface. The animal-like terminal is decorated with ears and eyes and has a pierced snout to hold a copper-alloy ring.

Although technically a strap-end, this class of object is now thought to have a more specialised function as a book fitting, largely due to the hole on the underside, which fitted onto a peg on the book's cover in order to secure it. A strap would have extended from the other cover of the book and slotted into the hollow end of the fitting. The ring at the end may have taken a cord to make it easier to pull the clasp on and off the peg.

Similar fittings can be found on books surviving from the medieval period and there is detail on a statue from the chapter house of St Mary's, York, to further support this theory. Such book fittings have been found in archaeological contexts of the late fourteenth and fifteenth centuries, many of them ecclesiastical, suggesting primary use in a religious setting.

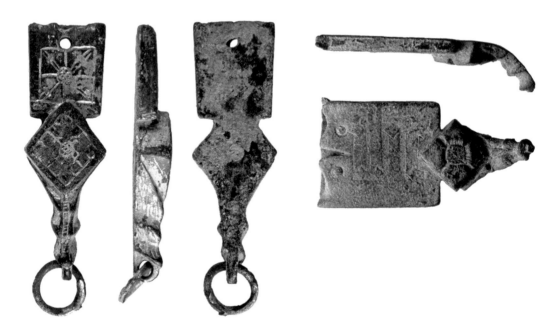

Left: A copper-alloy gilt book fitting from Hawkley.

Right: A similar book fitting from Norfolk with the inscription 'IhC', a variant of IHS, the first three letters of the name Jesus in Greek. (NMS-FD27A2)

43. Copper-alloy miniature book (HAMP527)
Medieval (AD 1200–1500)
Found in Bentley in 1997. Length 31 mm.

This miniature prayer book is a representation of the gospel of St Mark. It is modeled in the open position and engraved on two 'pages' with the Latin inscription PAX/TIBI/MAR/CE and EVAN/GELI/STA/MEUS. The reverse of the object is decorated with patches of small punched squares either side of the spine, which is decorated with transverse grooves in imitation of leather binding.

As legend has it, during St Mark's travels through Europe he stopped at Venice, where an angel appeared to him saying, 'Pax tibi, Marce evangelista meus' ('Peace be with you, Mark my evangelist'). This subsequently became the motto of Venice, its coat of arms depicting a winged lion, the symbol of St Mark, with its forepaw resting on the gospel. This representation of St Mark is seen in numerous locations around the city, the gospel inscribed with the motto above. Two of the most famous examples are on the Porta della Carta and the Basilica San Marco, although the representation is synonymous with St Mark and can be found across the world. Presumably this miniature book originally had a religious context and perhaps was part of a similar but smaller statue arrangement.

The finder has donated the object to the British Museum.

A medieval miniature prayer book from Bentley.

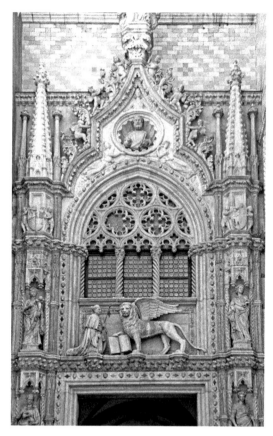

Left: The Porta della Carta – the entrance to the Palazzo Ducale, Venice. (Tony Hisgett via Wikimedia Commons)

Below: Detail of the lion and doge on the Porta della Carta. The lion rests his forepaw on the gospel of St Mark. (Greg Willis via Wikimedia Commons)

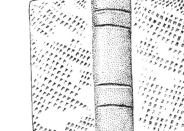

Right: A drawing of the miniature prayer book by Alan Cracknell.

Below: Detail of the façade of the Basilica San Marco in Venice, showing the lion with his forepaw on the gospel of St Mark. (QMeuh via Wikimedia Commons)

44. Copper-alloy seal matrix (HAMP-F31ED1)
Medieval (AD 1400–1500)
Found in Headbourne Worthy in 2004. Length 61.9 mm.

The practice of sealing a document in wax with your own mark became popular in the medieval period and, by the fourteenth century, stock designs and the use of lead meant that a seal matrix was within the grasp of the ordinary man or woman.

A pointed oval form of seal matrix like this one typically dates to the second half of the thirteenth century and is most common among women and the Church. To the reverse is a pierced lug, which both ensured a good thumb grip and also allowed the matrix to be suspended around the neck or from a belt.

The central motif is an engraved image of the Virgin Mary offering her breast to the infant Jesus beneath an elaborate canopy, with rays of light appearing to surround them. A lily pot stands to either side of the niche, the lily being a symbol of the Virgin Mary. The legend around reads SIGILLUM OFFICII PRIORIS DE PULLA ('the official seal of the Priory of Pill'), and is punctuated by sprigs of foliage.

Pill Priory, dedicated jointly to the Blessed Virgin Mary and St Budoc, is located just outside Milford Haven in Pembrokeshire. It was founded in the late twelfth century as a satellite house of the Roman Catholic Abbey of Tiron in northern France, itself an order of reformed Benedictine monks. Pill Priory is incomplete today, but the chancel arch and south transept survive and are designated as scheduled ancient monuments by Cadw.

The find has been donated to Pill Priory.

Medieval seal matrix from Headbourne Worthy.

Right: An imprinted seal using the matrix from Headbourne Worthy.

Below: A seal matrix from Horndean, which translates as the seal of Hugh the Collier (maker or seller of charcoal) or perhaps alternatively the Student. (HAMP-0C98EC)

Chapter 7
Later Hampshire

Hampshire's later period sees much change. While the cities of Southampton and Winchester dwindle in importance, Portsmouth rises swiftly to the fore in response to the martial threat from France and Henry VIII's great warship, the *Mary Rose,* is built. Elsewhere, Hampshire remains largely agricultural while smaller towns such as Alton, Andover, Basingstoke, Romsey and Petersfield grow and flourish. The Dissolution of the Monasteries meant that religious establishments now passed into the hands of landowners, many of whom either rebuilt or converted them into large stately homes, including, for example, Mottisfont Abbey, Titchfield Abbey, The Vyne and Highclere Castle.

Finds from this post-medieval period largely comprise coinage and dress accessories, such as buckles, pins, dress hooks and belt-mounts. Finds of pottery are more common in this period too, often reflecting the products of the north-east Hampshire kilns, namely 'Border Ware' and 'Tudor Green' wares: red and white fabrics with green, yellow and brown glazes.

The Civil War, known in Hampshire for its battle and skirmishes (for example, at Basing House, Cheriton and Alton), is also visible through finds of musket balls and associated paraphernalia. Where lead shot can be precisely recorded to within 1 metre of its recovery, the data can be invaluable in gauging the location and direction of a battle. It is, therefore, extremely important that such finds have an accurate findspot.

Water meadows begin to shape the landscape at this time, followed by improved roads, canals and eventually railways. The maritime importance of the Solent area can be seen with the continuing development of Portsmouth and Buckler's Hard in the eighteenth century. While we tend not to record items dating from after 1700, if finds of particular interest turn up, they are noted, as demonstrated by the examples below.

A body sherd of a 'Tudor Green' ware ceramic vessel from Greater London, with ribbed decoration on the outside. (LON-921D88)

Cheriton: view of the battlefield looking south with an interpretative panel in the foreground. The Battle of Cheriton took place in 1644 and was an important win for the Parliamentarians. (Katie Hinds)

Lead shot, probably for use in a carbine, from Penton Grafton. Diameter 19.3 mm. (HAMP-550EF3)

A cap from a lead powder measure, which would have fastened to the bandolier (belt) with a cord. The flask itself would have contained enough explosive for a complete charge for the weapon. A series of twelve of these holders and caps would have been attached to the bandolier. From Amport. (HAMP-CoB276)

45. Silver gilt coin (HAMP-8D0E55)
Post-Medieval (AD 1561)
Found in Chilcomb in 2011. Diameter 19.7 mm.

Originally silver, this coin of Elizabeth I has been modified by the addition of gilding to both surfaces. However, unlike find no. 34 (the Saxon coin brooch), there are no signs of attachment for a pin, or a piercing for suspension, and the coin has been gilded entirely on both surfaces – not something you would need to do if only one side was intended to be seen. Shakespeare's Falstaff refers to his companions as 'gilt twopences' in *Henry IV Part II*, saying that he overshines them; this suggests that the forgery of gold coins was a known practice at the time.

It seems likely then that this threepence was intended to pass as a gold coin; the most similar in size is the issue known as the *crown*, and the use of the same obverse (head side) die for both silver and gold issues of the same size was not uncommon. Presumably, if the receiver was not looking too closely, it would be an easy deception.

There is only a handful of gilded Elizabethan coins on the PAS database, suggesting that the practice was not common. This coin was minted at the Tower of London in 1561 and bears the legends ELIZABETH D G ANG FRA ET HI REGINA ('Elizabeth, by the grace of God, Queen of England, France and Ireland') and POSVI DEV ADIVTOREM MEV ('I have made God my helper'). The date is recorded on the reverse.

Silver gilt coin of Elizabeth I from Chilcomb.

For comparison, a gold crown of Elizabeth I from near Fordingbridge. (WILT-E683B3)

46. Lead cloth seal (HAMP-19B0F2)
Post-Medieval (AD 1550–1650)
Found in Sutton Scotney in 2008. Diameter 27.9 mm.

As mentioned previously, cloth seals are an official tag relating to the length, breadth and quality of a piece of cloth. Usually they were in two parts or discs, with a connecting strip that folded around the edge of the cloth and a rivet behind one disc piercing the cloth so that, when squashed together with the second disc, the authentication was sealed with the material between. They are quite common finds from the sixteenth and seventeenth century.

This example originated in the Low Countries and is incomplete. The front of the surviving disc depicts a haloed St Peter holding a key in each hand with the legend S[....]PEETER, probably 'St' Peter. The representation of St Peter and the Low Germanic spelling help identify this cloth seal as having originated in Turnhout (modern Belgium), a city renowned at this time for its linen textiles.

While the lack of a second disc might initially be considered a disappointment, it is actually a stroke of luck, as the object holds hidden information on the reverse of the disc, which would not be visible had both discs survived. What is revealed is the zig-zag imprint of striped twill, the fabric to which the seal was once attached. It was a light fabric and probably used for bedding. Evidence such as this is invaluable, given that the material itself is very unlikely to survive.

A similar cloth seal has been recorded from Newport, Isle of Wight. This find has been donated to Hampshire Cultural Trust, formerly Winchester Museums Service.

A post-medieval lead cloth seal from Sutton Scotney.

A cloth seal from Norfolk bearing the arms of the city of Norwich on one side and, on the other, the inscription TO / NARO / WE in three lines, indicating that the cloth was narrower than the regulation stipulated by the 'alnage' system of quality control. (NMS-3043C5)

89

47. Gold bracelet slide (HAMP-841BCo)
Post-Medieval (AD 1706)
Found in Kingsclere in 2013. Length 20.6 mm.

This very personal object offers a direct connection with the past. It is a *memento mori*, something to remind us of our own mortality and often coupled as remembrance for someone who has died. The idea of *memento mori*, which translates from Latin as 'remember to die' but is interpreted as 'remember you must die', captured the imagination from the Middle Ages onwards, bolstered by the church. Examples of uncomfortable images associated with death can be seen in art and architecture, as well as in music and literature.

This object is a bracelet slide and would have been worn on a ribbon around the wrist (a clasp and pin are missing). On the underside, not visible when worn, is the inscription: E B / Dyed aprill / 21 1706 / aged 38. On the visible front is a rock crystal setting, now damaged. Beneath this can be seen gold thread, patches of red and hints of other colours – probably the remains of an image of the deceased in enamel and gold thread.

The object was acquired by Hampshire Cultural Trust after being declared Treasure.

Gold bracelet slide from Kingsclere.

A gold finger ring inscribed MEMENTO MORI and missing a white enamel skull setting at the centre, from the Isle of Wight. (IOW-9E6B77)

A copper-alloy knife handle, from Greater London, on a *memento mori* theme, with the inscription RD 1598. It features a human figure on one side and a skeleton on the other, with a winged demon above. (LON-CE5FD7)

This unusual coin is a base-silver threepence struck by the colony of Massachusetts in North America. It has been pierced, suggesting secondary use perhaps as jewellery.

The coin is of the 'pine tree' type after the image on the obverse. The legend surrounding it reads MASATHVSETS, while the reverse legend reads NEW ENGLAND around a central date 1652 and denomination III over two lines.

There are only four other coins of this type on the PAS database and, although all known examples are dated 1652, it is generally accepted that they were in fact issued later between 1667 and 1674. The earlier date perhaps commemorates the foundation of a Massachusetts mint. The coin is symbolic of a time when people in overseas colonies felt they could legitimately issue coinage, which was usually the prerogative of the king.

A silver threepence struck by the colony of Massachusetts, from Stubbington.

One of the other four 'pine tree' Massachusetts coins on the PAS database. This one is a shilling from Cheshire. (LVPL-1CFD55)

49. Copper-alloy coins (HAMP-E4E185)
Post-Medieval (AD 1711)
Found in Bishop's Waltham in 2010. Average diameter 25 mm.

Discovered under the floorboards of a shop, this hoard of 7,083 coins raises some intriguing questions. Many of the coins had suffered from corrosion and were difficult to read, and so in the first instance a 10 per cent sample was chosen for identification. A second random control sample of 100 coins was also chosen for identification (as far as was possible) and both groups turned up remarkably similar results: all coins that were identifiable were from the mint of Lyon (shown by the mintmark 'D') and all coins with a readable date were 1711.

The coins are apparently 30 *denier* pieces issued by Louis XIV of France, of a billon denomination (composed of copper alloy and silver) struck only at Metz and Lyon. These coins were not intended as currency in France, though – they were for export to the French colonies of Canada and Louisiana.

Closer inspection revealed these coins to be contemporary forgeries of the 30 *denier* piece, albeit good ones, and their general consistency in size and weight suggests that they may have been made using official dies. So what were they doing hidden under a Hampshire floor?

Could it be the coins were a failed attempt by the English to infiltrate the French economy? Or perhaps they were seized at the Port of Southampton on their way from Lyon to North America. Unfortunately it is unlikely we will ever know the true story, and why they ended up in Bishop's Waltham.

The obverse of the coins has the legend LVD XIIII FR ET NAV REX ('Louis XIIII, King of France and Navarre'), while the reverse reads PIECE DE XXX DENIERS D ('30 deniers piece, D – for Lyon').

A hoard from Bishop's
Waltham of Louis XIV
30 *denier* pieces.

One of the clearer coins after professional cleaning. The wear at the centre of both sides is from a worn die and is not wear on the coin itself.

This image shows the vast differences in flan size, suggestive of a counterfeit operation.

50. Silver coin (SUR-D2D574)
Modern (AD 1911–19)
Found in Nether Wallop in 2014. Diameter 22.5 mm.

This coin is a florin of George V and was issued between 1911 and 1919. It was in the process of being adapted to form a finger ring when it was lost – or possibly the project was abandoned. Adapting a coin in this manner is a relatively affordable way of making a silver ring and seems to have been common. Indeed, during this particular period, when we see a number of these finger rings fashioned in this way, it is thought that the process was a form of 'trench art', produced by soldiers away at war.

The edges of the coin have been hammered inwards so that the object takes on an H-shape in cross-section. The central part would then have been drilled out to leave the outer edge only. The inscription GEORGIVS V DG BRITT OMN REX FD IND IMP ('George V, by the grace of God, king of all Britons, defender of the faith, emperor of India') can still be read and the bust is clearly visible.

Above: Another coin finger ring: a silver shilling of George VI, diameter 25 mm, with the inside irregularly cut-out. From Hursley. (HAMP-8F4391)

Left: A George V florin finger ring from Nether Wallop.

Some Useful Online Resources

Below are a number of useful websites for further research into archaeological finds and Hampshire's archaeology.

Hampshire's Archaeology and Historic Buildings Record – www3.hants.gov.uk
Southampton Historic Environment Record – www.southampton.gov.uk
Winchester Historic Environment Record – www.winchester.gov.uk
Portsmouth Historic Environment Record – www.portsmouthcitymuseums.co.uk
Hampshire Cultural Trust Online Collections – www.hampshireculturaltrust.org.uk/content/collections-online
Hampshire Field Club & Archaeological Society – www.hantsfieldclub.org.uk
Council for British Archaeology (Wessex) – www.cba-wessex.org.uk
The Portable Antiquities Scheme – www.finds.org.uk
Later Prehistoric Finds Group – https://sites.google.com/site/laterprehistoricfindsgroup
Roman Finds Group – www.romanfindsgroup.org.uk
Finds Research Group – www.findsresearchgroup.com